I Walk with Angels

THE LIFE AND WORK
OF JAMES ENGEL

Carl R. Ziebell

Lutheran University Press
Minneapolis, Minnesota

I Walk with Angels
The Life and Work of James Engel

Carl R. Ziebell, author

This monograph is adapted from a research project submitted in partial fulfillment of the requirements for the Master of Church Music Degree, Concordia University Mequon, Wisconsin. April 13, 2011.

Published under the auspices of:
Center for Church Music
Concordia University Chicago
River Forest, IL 60305-1402

ISBN: 978-1-942304-35-7

Lutheran University Press
Minneapolis, MN 55439
Manufactured in the United States of America

Contents

About the Center
for Church Music

The Center for Church Music was established in 2010 on the campus of Concordia University Chicago. Its purpose is to provide ongoing research and educational resources in Lutheran church music, especially in the areas of congregational song and composition for the Church. It is intended to be of interest to pastors, musicians, and laity alike.

The Center maintains a continually expanding resource room that houses the Schalk American Lutheran Hymnal Collection, the manuscript collections of prominent Lutheran composers and hymn writers, and a broad array of reference works and resources in church music. To create a global awareness and facilitate online research, efforts are underway to digitize the hymnal collection, the manuscript archives, and the hymn festival recordings.

The Center publishes monographs and books covering various aspects of Lutheran church music.

The Center maintains a dynamic website whose features include devotions, presentations, oral histories, biographical essays, resource recommendations, and conversations on various topics in worship and church music.

The Center's Founders Group includes Linda and Robert Kempke, Nancy and Bill Raabe, Mary and Charles Sukup, and Waldemar B. Seefeldt, whose significant monetary gifts initiated the Center and have, along with the gifts of many others, sustained its momentum.

The Center's Advisory Board includes James Freese, Scott Hyslop, Linda Kempke, Jonathan Kohrs, Nancy Raabe, Carl Schalk, Steven Wente, and Paul Westermeyer.

Barry L. Bobb serves as the Center's volunteer director.

You can follow news about the Center on Facebook. Learn more about the Center and subscribe to its free e-newsletter at http://cuchicago.edu/about-concordia/center-for-church-music

Acknowledgements

The author wishes to thank everyone who helped him along this journey. Special thanks go to:

. . . members of the Engel family:
† Norma Engel (widow of James Engel),
Janet Engel (sister of James Engel),
†Mary Geis and Joan Mueller (daughters of James Engel);

. . . Dr. Richard Wegner (classmate and colleague of James Engel), who spent many hours helping the author learn about Engel's early life and giving the author much needed advice;

. . . and the many students and colleagues of Engel who contributed to this paper.

Further acknowledgement goes to Dr. James Freese, the author's advisor, for all of his patient help, guidance, and technical assistance; and Dr. David Eggebrecht (archivist for Concordia University Wisconsin) for bringing his research and writing expertise to bear on this project.

Introduction

The history of the Lutheran Church is replete with excellent and noteworthy musicians, hymnists and composers. When one thinks of Lutheran music through the years, we certainly recall the work of J.S. Bach (1685-1750), Dietrich Buxtehude (c. 1637-1707), and other beloved Lutheran musicians. In the mid-20th century, we have had a wealth of Lutheran musicians, a special generation who enhanced and changed Lutheran worship for the better. Paul Manz (1919-2009), Carl Schalk, (b. 1929), and Walter Pelz (b. 1926) are just a few of the renowned members of that generation and are treasured by church musicians throughout the United States and beyond.

James Engel (1925-1989) was a part of that generation and played an important role in the history of Lutheran church music. Engel was known by his colleagues and students as an excellent musician, choir director, composer and teacher. He had a positive influence on the next generation of Lutheran musicians. In his later years, he became well-known as a composer of church music. His organ and choral works have been performed by many musicians through the years. One of Engel's signature choral works is titled *I Walk with Angels*. Indeed, he lived his Christian faith and walked with angels throughout his life. The title of this exploration of his life and work is therefore fitting—*I Walk with Angels: The Life and Work of James Engel*.

Very little has been written about James Engel. The author was able to find small summaries and biographical program notes about him, but the majority of the research done for this paper was accomplished through letters, email correspondence, personal interviews and research in the archives of Concordia University Wisconsin, and Martin Luther College, New Ulm, MN. This paper provides a detailed biography of Engel's life, provides insight into his character, highlights his musical work and presents a music catalog of his work.

Carl R. Ziebell

James Engel

Biographical Background

Growing Up in Milwaukee

James Edward Engel was born in Milwaukee, Wisconsin on March 21, 1925.[1] His parents were Carl and Emma (née Eggert) Engel.[2] As his wife, Mrs. Norma Engel, noted, this was the 240th anniversary of J. S. Bach's birth. This was fortuitous since Engel was destined to become a musician. In fact, Mrs. Engel commented further that his godmother—Anna Bernardine Dorothy Hoppe[3] —prayed before his birth that he would be a musician.[4]

Engel was born into a large family. He had three brothers and four sisters. (See Appendix A—Engel family picture.) Mary Geis, one of Engel's daughters, recalls her aunts and uncles to be a "joyous" group of people, and that Engel brought this joy into his own household when he had a family of his own. Since Engel's family was large, the boys shared one bedroom and the girls shared another.

Geis recalls her dad telling her about how his mother used to sing hymns to him when he was a little boy. "She had them memorized and would sing when she ironed."[5] Mary mentioned that she had asked her father about this and wondered if this might be where he developed his love of music. "He told me that he indeed carried those melodies in his heart from that time forward."[6]

Engel also told Mary how much he appreciated his mother's faith in the Lord. He indicated that she lived her faith and was an example for her children. Engel would later follow his mother and father's faithful example and live a life devoted to his Lord and Savior. These events in his early life were essential in providing Engel a model that he eventually passed down to his own children and the students whom he taught. "Train up a child in the way he should go, and when he is old he will not turn from it." (Proverbs 22:6)

Engel began taking piano lessons at an early age. Piano lessons at that time cost the Engel family $2 per semester for each student. His family had a piano in their house, and he and his brothers and sisters learned how to play it.[7] Engel continued taking piano lessons through his high school years.[8]

Engel attended Bethlehem Lutheran School, which was located in a neighborhood a little west of the downtown Milwaukee area. Bethlehem school was founded in 1884, and was located just west of Bethlehem Lutheran Church at the corner of W. McKinley and 24th Street. In 1930, when he was old enough, Engel's parents enrolled him into Bethlehem's kindergarten class, but his teachers soon realized that he could read already and transferred him into the first grade.[9] The growing school had an enrollment of 200 students at that time.[10] (See Appendix B—Bethlehem Lutheran School.)

The Engel family lived on 25th Street, between Vliet Street and McKinley Avenue, not far from Bethlehem Lutheran Church. Engel's sister, Janet, gives us a glimpse into his childhood.

The first episode describes a rich family life with the Engel children at play.

> There was a vacant lot next door to our house on 25th Street—a nice playground for a family of eight kids. It served as a baseball field in the summers (with a few broken windows), and Dad made an ice skating rink out of it in the winter.[11]

As with many families, the Engels periodically went to visit family who lived beyond the city of Milwaukee or would take a drive out to a lake to swim and enjoy nature. Janet Engel tells a story about one of those trips to the lake:

> Many Sunday afternoons in summer we'd drive out to Silver Lake (Oconomowoc) to swim. Mom's brother had a home there and her sisters and brothers would congregate there. One Sunday, Mom was embarrassed because Jim hadn't gotten a haircut and it was just a little long. She decided it needed to be cut and proceeded to do so sitting in the back seat and bump, bump, bumping all the way. I'm not too sure which was better, the before or after!![12]

Engel was the best of friends with Richard Wegner who lived on 23rd Street, near the corner of Lisbon Avenue, just five blocks away from the Engel family. Richard Wegner grew up with Engel and followed a similar life path. They belonged to the Bethlehem Lutheran Church and played on the church's softball team.[13] As Wegner recalled, he and his brother Henry, along with Engel and one of his brothers, comprised the infield of the team.[14]

Engel and Wegner went to Concordia Teachers College in River Forest, Illinois together and both became teachers, notable Lutheran musicians and composers. Wegner is currently organist and music director *emeritus* at Immanuel Lutheran Church in Baltimore, Maryland.

Engel and Wegner were confirmed at Bethlehem Lutheran Church by Pastor Oscar Kaiser on Sunday, April 10, 1938.[15] After graduating from Bethlehem Lutheran School in 1938, Engel went on to attend Lutheran High School in Milwaukee.[16] The school's building where he attended was located at the corner of 13th and Reservoir Street. The enrollment of LHS when Engel started attending in 1938 was approximately 265 students. However, the enrollment at LHS was growing by almost 100 students a year during those years, and by the time he was a senior, space was already getting tight at the school.[17]

Undergraduate Studies at Concordia Teachers College, River Forest, Illinois

After Engel graduated from LHS in 1942, he went on to attend Concordia Teachers College in River Forest, Illinois. He was the first member of his family to go to college. In September of 1942, Engel and Wegner boarded a train together for Chicago and River Forest. Little did they realize at the time that their musical lives would run a parallel course. They attended Concordia together for three years and for a fourth year as instructors in piano and organ. Wegner commented that freshmen were not able to choose their roommates. "We were the servants of the seniors during that first year. We cleaned the rooms and did all of the nonsense things."[18] After that initial year however, students could choose their roommates. Engel and Wegner were roommates from 1943-1946. Mrs. Engel commented that James went to Concordia with the intent of becoming a math teacher and he did utilize that background when he taught at Fox Valley Lutheran High School. However, music ultimately became the primary focus of his career.[19]

At that time, due to World War II, Concordia's students went to school during the summer. Wegner recalls that the leadership of the Lutheran Church—Missouri Synod and the U.S. government came to an agreement allowing Concordia's students to be deferred (4D class).

As a result Concordia's teacher track students received the same deferment as divinity students. As part of this deferment, the college was to hold summer sessions during the war years. Engel and Wegner attended these summer sessions, called the Summer Quarter, at Concordia in 1944 and 1945, allowing them to graduate in three years instead of the standard four-year term.[20]

In 1944 Engel and Wegner studied organ with Dr. Carl Halter, who was the organist at Grace Lutheran Church near the campus of Concordia.[21] In 1945-46, Engel and Richard Wegner both studied with Frederick Marriott who was the organist at Rockefeller Chapel on the campus of the University of Chicago. Marriott held that post from 1932-1953. He also played the chapel's carillon. Marriott had been a student of Marcel Dupré (1886-1971), a noted organist, recitalist and composer from France. It is also interesting to note that both Engel and Wegner, as students of Fred Marriott, played organ recitals at Rockefeller Chapel on the great E. M. Skinner organ[22] that was housed there. "We both turned pages for each other," Wegner recalls.[23]

Besides his organ studies, Engel studied music composition with Professor Irwin Fischer in Chicago. Wegner recalls that Engel would travel to downtown Chicago and take composition lessons with Fischer on Saturdays.[24] Fischer was a professor at the American Conservatory of Music in Chicago. He was a noted American composer and conductor and had studied composition with famous composers such as Zoltán Kodály (1882-1967) and Nadia Boulanger (1887-1979).

One of the interesting facts that Wegner mentioned was that while he was a student, many of the important Lutheran organ scholars were friends in college and at the university. It was this generation of musicians that greatly influenced the music of the Lutheran church and guided it to where it is today. According to Wegner, a number of these musicians also studied with Fred Marriott and Carl Halter. They had a collegial attitude towards each other and would go out of their way to study together and help each other out. It was not the competitive atmosphere that one might imagine. The only thing they really competed for was organ practice time, which was at a premium.[25]

While studying at Concordia, Engel played for worship services at First Zion Evangelical Lutheran Church, located in Chicago at 19th and Peoria.[26] The congregation was of German background and still held services in German. Mrs. Engel recalled that the pastor used to signal him whenever he was supposed to play something since he did not understand the language. He also directed the choir at this church but they sang the anthems in English.[27]

Engel graduated from Concordia, River Forest in 1945 at age 20. At the time there was a shortage of organ and piano teachers at Concordia. Engel and Richard Wegner stayed on as organ and piano instructors for an extra year to help reduce the effects of the teacher shortage.

Wegner recalls an incident soon after he and Engel graduated from Concordia. They had a long talk with Martin Hasz, Engel's future father-in-law. He gave Richard Wegner and Engel a great amount of advice about teaching. "He gave us all kinds of helpful suggestions."[28] Mary Geis commented that her grandfather was a wonderful man and very hospitable.[29] One can imagine that they put all of his advice and suggestions to good use in their own teaching careers.

Teaching and Making Music While Serving Bethlehem Lutheran Church and School in Milwaukee

In 1946 Engel accepted a call to his home congregation of Bethlehem Lutheran Church and School in Milwaukee, Wisconsin. Since he was a "son of the congregation," it was logical that he would receive a call there sometime during his ministry. Mrs. Engel said that he received this call because he was well-known and respected at Bethlehem.

She also indicated that he was happy that Bethlehem was his initial call so that he could serve there first and then move on to new fields of service.[30] While at Bethlehem, he taught 5th and 6th grade and served in the church's music program. Engel served in the teaching and music ministry at Bethlehem Lutheran Church and School for two years. (See Appendix B—Bethlehem Lutheran Church.)

The organ that Engel played is still there and in working condition, although it has been rebuilt and expanded a couple of times through the years. Much of the information that follows is from a church handout provided by Pastor Micah Wildauer. Bethlehem Lutheran's organ was built by William Schuelke in 1888. The Schuelke Organ Company was well-known throughout the Midwest during the late 1800s—early 1900s. While there are very few Schuelke organs that have survived into the 21st century, a few still exist. The Bethlehem instrument is one of three Schuelke organs that are known to still be in service within the city of Milwaukee. The other two Schuelke instruments are located at Historic Trinity Lutheran Church (destroyed by fire in 2018) in Downtown Milwaukee and St. Francis Roman Catholic Church. At the time that Engel was playing the instrument, the organ was reported to have sixteen ranks. The organ had been rebuilt in 1935, eleven years before Engel took the call to serve at Bethlehem. The console was moved to different locations around the balcony during the organ's history but has returned to the center where it currently resides. (See Appendix C—Bethlehem's Schuelke Organ.)

It was during Engel's tenure at Bethlehem School that he married Norma Hasz (1925-2009). They met when they were both students at Concordia, River Forest. He and Norma were married at St. Paul's Evangelical Lutheran Church in Mt. Prospect, Illinois, on July 12, 1947. Pastor J. E. A. Mueller officiated at their wedding.[31]

It was somewhere in this time period that Engel's father died. Mary Geis commented that her dad was in his 20s when his father died. His father had been in the "chicken business" in Milwaukee. The part of the chicken business in which Engel's father worked is not known. Nonetheless, according to Wegner and Geis, Engel's father worked with chickens.[32] His work provided enough money so that he and his wife could provide a good and loving home for Engel and his brothers and sisters.

Wegner mentioned that during the summer of 1947, he and Engel attended the Christiansen Choral School, which was held that year in

Lake Forest, Illinois. These annual summer institutes were started in 1935 and were intended for American choral directors.[33] The school promoted the choral style of Professors F. Melius Christiansen and Olaf Christiansen from St.. Olaf College in Northfield, Minnesota. Dr. Paul Manz (1919-2009), one of the most famous Lutheran composers of the 20th-century, also attended this event that summer and posed for a picture with Engel. The photograph was taken by Wegner who told the author the story behind this picture. (See Appendix A—Engel and Paul Manz in the summer of 1947.)

> You will never guess what Jim, Paul Manz and I did this day. We took off from the Christiansen Choral School. We got tired so we all got into Paul Manz's car. It was a pretty nice car. One of the three, I didn't suggest it, said, "Let's go play golf today." So we went out on the golf course for four hours in the sunshine.[34]

During the summers of 1946 and 1948, Marcel Dupré (1886-1971) came to Chicago and presented weekly Wednesday evening recitals at Rockefeller Chapel, University of Chicago (The very Chapel where Engel and Wegner had studied organ years before).[35] Richard Wegner went to many of those recitals and recalls taking the Engels along with him to one of Marcel Dupre's recitals. "I remember driving them from Milwaukee in 1948 to the recital that night. I remember how sleepy I was driving home up Highway 41."[36] It was a slower journey between Chicago and Milwaukee in those days because the interstate system and the TriState Tollway had not yet been constructed.

During his years at Bethlehem, Engel took organ lessons from Hugo Gehrke (1912- 1992). Gehrke was also Richard Wegner's first superior organ teacher.[37] Gehrke was a well-known and respected composer, professor and organist. He served many years as a teacher and director of music at Immanuel Lutheran Church in Milwaukee. Gehrke was serving Immanuel at the time when Engel was taking organ lessons from him but took a call to teach music at Concordia College in Oakland, California in 1950.[38]

Singing with the Lutheran A Cappella Choir of Milwaukee

Engel became involved in the music program of the Lutheran A Cappella Choir of Milwaukee in 1947. (See Appendix A—Lutheran A Cappella Choir.) The choir was founded in 1937 by Gerhard Schroth and has become well-known and respected throughout southeastern Wisconsin and beyond. It is worth noting that Gerhard Schroth directed the church choir at Bethlehem Lutheran Church (Engel's home congregation) during the time that he also directed the Lutheran A Cappella Choir. The Lutheran A Cappella Choir is still active today after more than seventy years of singing.[39]

Engel worked with the Lutheran A Cappella Choir through the years in a variety of different roles. He started with the choir as a tenor. He accompanied the choir at the organ for certain concerts and was listed as the assistant director in some of the concert programs from 1957-1960.[40] The author had the opportunity to talk with Suzanne Eggold, longtime member of the choir and current choir librarian.[41] Upon looking through the choir's programs through the years, one can see the extent of Engel's involvement. Hugo Gehrke was the director of the choir at that time.[42] Engel was first listed as a tenor in the May 25, 1947 concert program. He is again listed in the December and spring concert programs of the 1947-48 season.[43] It was during that summer that Engel accepted the call to serve St. John Lutheran Church and School in Racine, Wisconsin.

In the fall of 1950, Harold Albers took over the baton from Gehrke. For the winter and spring concerts of 1952, Engel was noted in concert programs as playing the organ. In the January 28, 1952 concert held at Holy Ghost Lutheran Church, he was listed as playing the voluntary. For the "Service of Easter Music" in 1952, Engel is listed as playing the organ for Bach's Cantata #4.[44] Richard Wegner informs us: "My brother, Henry Wegner, played violin in this concert."[45] For Easter 1953, three organists, including Engel, were listed in the program. However, who played what piece was not indicated. He is again listed as organist in the 1955 and 1956 "Service of Easter Music" programs. Engel reprised his role as accompanist for Bach's Easter cantata a number of times through the 1950s and 60s. Dr. Fred Bartel, a colleague from Dr. Martin Lutheran College and former student of Gehrke's, recalls that along with accompanying Bach's Easter cantata, *Christ lag in Todesbanden*, Engel played the Easter chorale preludes from Bach's *Orgelbüchlein*.[46] Dr. Edward Meyer recalls attending these concerts in the early 1960s when he lived in Milwaukee. "Those concerts were absolutely outstanding, of the finest work. The performance of [Cantata No. 4] was always an event."[47] These Easter concerts were a tradition for the choir and were held at Immanuel Lutheran Church for many years. This congregation was one of the largest LCMS congregations in the Milwaukee metropolitan area in those days. Immanuel was known to have a fine three-manual Wangerin pipe organ and it was on this instrument that Engel accompanied the Lutheran A Cappella Choir.

At the time Engel joined the choir, it was primarily an a cappella choir as the name suggests. However the organ and other instruments were used for certain pieces. Richard Wegner recalls that his brother, Henry, played the violin on numerous occasions. He is listed many times in the "Service of Easter Music" through the years. He also sang in the Lutheran A Cappella Choir for many years as did Richard Wegner before he moved out east.[48] This fact is interesting since it was not common to have other instruments, besides the organ, accompany choral concerts in Lutheran churches during the 1940s into the 1960s.[49] Today, other instruments are commonly used to accompany choirs and congregations in the Lutheran Church, much as it was common during J. S. Bach's lifetime.

Engel is noted in the Christmas 1957 program as the assistant choir director. This corresponded with his return to Milwaukee as music professor at Concordia. He is listed in the Easter 1958 program as the assistant director and as a choir member. As part of the choir's archive, Engel is listed as the director of the mass male chorus at the Third Annual Lutheran Intercollegiate Choral Festival. He was listed as the assistant director and choir member in the Christmas 1958 program and only listed as a choir member in the spring 1959 concert. In the 1959 Christmas program, Engel was listed as the assistant choir director and a choir member. He also played the harpsichord for this concert. He continued as assistant director through 1960 and is not listed as such again. Also in 1960, the Lutheran A Cappella Choir started having guest organists play at their concerts on a more regular basis. Engel continued to play the organ for the choir periodically throughout the 1960s.

In the fall of 1966, Eldon Balko, from Concordia College, became the director of the choir. Engel remained involved with the choir as organ accompanist. Under the direction of Balko, Engel played for two special events that were noted in the choir archives. These were when Engel played for the Lutheran Hour Rally at the Milwaukee Auditorium in June, 1967 and when he played the organ dedication at Hales Corners Lutheran Church in 1968.

Teaching and Making Music While Serving
St. John Lutheran Church and School, Racine, WI

In 1948 Engel took a call to serve St. John Evangelical Lutheran Church and School in Racine, Wisconsin. He was to be the fifth and sixth grade teacher for the school, as well as the organist and choir director for the church.[50] St. John congregation still maintains the school to this day, but the old school building that he taught in has since been replaced with a newer building. (See Appendix B—St. John Lutheran Church.)

Wegner recalls an interesting fact: "In 1947 I was called to St. John, Racine. In 1948, Jim was called to that church. I declined the call in '47. He accepted it in '48."[51] Along with the current organist and choral director, Arthur Preuss, it is obvious to this author that the leadership of St. John Lutheran Church in Racine has historically shown a desire for quality Lutheran music and has made it a priority to call the best musicians available to lead its program.

As a result of calling fine musicians to St. John Lutheran Church, young people of the congregation were exposed to quality church music. One of these students was Dr. Donald Busarow (1934-2011). Busarow was a well-known organist and professor of music at Wittenberg College in Springfield, Ohio. He was widely known for his musical compositions and hymn festival presentations. As previously mentioned, Engel came to St. John Lutheran Church in the fall of 1948. Busarow started high school that same year and took organ lessons from Engel.[52] His recollections best speak for themselves:

Jim was our organist and choir director at St. John's Lutheran Church in Racine, WI. I started high school in

'48 and I was already interested in the organ through our previous organist, Leslie Zeddies, who was my 3rd- and 4th-grade teacher. I was sure by the time Jim came that I would be going to [River Forest] to prepare for the same kind of profession. Jim agreed to help me during my junior and senior years of high school.

We had lessons on an irregular basis because of high school activities, but often enough to get me into the "Little Eight" of J.S. Bach along with service playing. I remember playing for him when he would go downstairs for communion. The story I often tell about church music in those days was that it was "endless." The service was filled with bridges and modulations to cover every moment. So, when Jim was about to leave the bench, I would slide on from the other side. He is sounding a chord with one hand and my hand would climb on top of his, he would slide out and I was on my own. The next thing the people knew was that he's downstairs partaking of the sacrament and we haven't missed a beat! I'd then continue the hymn being sung. He'd return and repeat the process from the other side. Shortly after I began my work at RF in '52, Jim took the position at Concordia College, Milwaukee.[53]

The organ at St. John's Lutheran Church while Engel taught there was a Kilgen instrument. The author had the opportunity to talk with Arthur Preuss, who succeeded Engel as a teacher and the music director at St. John's in 1957, and has served the congregation for over fifty years. The Kilgen organ was installed in 1919, but by the time Preuss first saw it, the organ was in great need of repair. A year after he arrived, he suggested that the organ be replaced and designed the present Schlicker instrument. Preuss earned his Master's degree from Northwestern University with an emphasis in organ design, so he was perfect for the task.[54] The current instrument was dedicated in 1961. (See Appendix C— Kilgen and Schlicker organs at St. John Lutheran Church.)

While he lived in Racine, Engel attended Northwestern University in Evanston, Illinois. Northwestern University had long been known for its excellent school of music. It was there, in 1951, where he earned his Master of Music degree. Mrs. Dorothy Croll, who grew up at St. John Lutheran Church in Racine, recalls a conversation she had with him on the day he took his comprehensive exam at Northwestern. She was taking lessons from him at the time and had a lesson on the day he took the exam.

> He had just come back from taking his master's exam. He said that he was amazed that they didn't just ask him about music; they asked him about everything. It was very broad.[55]

It is also interesting to note that when Croll later moved to Baltimore, she studied the organ with Wegner.

After Engel earned his master's degree, he taught piano part-time for several years at the Racine College of Music.[56] During this time, he had the opportunity to play the organ with the Racine Symphony Orchestra "at a pops concert in Memorial Hall in 1957."[57] It was at this concert that he also played a piano duet with Grant Malme. Mrs. Engel commented that they played *The Carnival of the Animals* by Camille Saint-Saëns, and that they spent many hours together practicing for this performance.[58] Malme further added: "I remember we had two beautiful Steinway concert grand pianos, and I also remember it was fun to do and was well received by the large audience and the reviews in the newspaper." Malme also recalls that he and Engel played a "recital of works for two pianos at [Malme's] studio in Racine."[59] Malme and Engel continued to collaborate after he began teaching at Concordia, Milwaukee. They performed a duo-piano recital in the Milwaukee Concordia College Gymnasium on February 28, 1960. In the program were works by Bach, Brahms, Poulenc, Rachmaninoff and other composers.[60] (See Appendix A— Malme and Engel at the piano.) Malme is still a fixture in the Racine community and officially retired from teaching piano in May of 2007.[61]

Also during this time period, Engel had a musical association with Henry (Hank) Wegner. (See Appendix A—Henry Wegner and Engel.) Henry Wegner was Richard Wegner's brother and also a friend and musical colleague of Engel. Henry was known for being a choral conductor and an excellent violinist. He was the choral conductor first at Racine Lutheran High School in Racine, Wisconsin, and later at Lutheran High School in Milwaukee, Wisconsin, during this period in Engel's life. Croll commented that Henry started with "an almost non-existent choir" and developed the choral program at Racine Lutheran High School into a quality choral program.[62] Henry also founded the Racine Civic Choir. He often asked Engel to accompany the choir during its concerts. Richard Wegner also pointed out that many other choral conductors in the area became well aware of his fine piano accompaniment skills.[63] They often asked him to accompany their choirs during various concerts in the vicinity of Southeastern Wisconsin.

The young Engel family was blessed with four children while living in Racine. They had three girls and one boy. Kathleen was born in December of 1948; Mary in December of 1951; and the twins, James and Joan, in August of 1957.[64]

Life as a Music Professor at Concordia College, Milwaukee

In 1957 Engel received and accepted a call to serve as a music professor at Concordia High School and College in Milwaukee, Wisconsin. At this time, Concordia's College department was a two-year pre-seminary institution. As a result, it admitted only men. Professor Eldon Balko, from Concordia College in Milwaukee, commented that the pre-seminary students finished their training at Concordia Senior College in Fort Wayne, Indiana, before enrolling in one of the Missouri Synod's two seminaries.[65] Engel was involved with the music department of both the college and the high school.

There were many changes that occurred during the time Engel was a professor at Concordia. The school was already making institutional history when, in 1958, it reached 500 students.[66] The campus was at its physical capacity and still continued to grow. It grew "from seven acres to twenty-eight."[67] In the early 1960s, the college and high school departments became accredited by the North Central Association. The high school received accreditation in 1962 and the college in 1964.[68] All college institutions that wish to be official must be accredited by this agency. These evaluations take place periodically in an institution's life and require self-studies and the maintenance of high academic standards. Along with the self-study, Concordia looked at how it could expand its Milwaukee campus. In order to prepare for purchasing more land, the college engaged in a capital campaign.[69] Concordia College continued to grow and flourish.

From 1957-1965 Engel was the primary music teacher at Concordia. Balko goes so far as to say that he "was the 'music department'." Engel chaired Concordia's music department for fourteen years. He taught academic music courses, was the director of the men's chorus and taught organ lessons. As part of his duties, Engel performed at the organ for official college functions such as opening services and graduations.[70]

As director of the men's chorus at Concordia College, Engel undertook arranging Handel's *Messiah* so that it could be sung by the male chorus. Dorothy Croll recalls that her sister sang the female solos for the performance of *Messiah* when the male chorus sang it in concert.[71] The concert was performed in the college in the college gymnasium. Wegner recalls that the acoustics in that venue were "pretty good."[72] In the early 1960s Concordia College undertook a renovation of the chapel sanctuary. As a part of that project, a new organ was included in the plan. Engel was at the forefront of this project. Dr. Hugo Gehrke, who was a professor at Concordia College in Oakland, California, at that time, undertook the design of the Concordia instrument. As previously mentioned, Gehrke was an important figure in Engel's musical development. Gehrke was known for his love of the neo-baroque tracker organ and was involved in the design of a number of tracker instruments around the country. Richard Wegner commented that Gehrke also designed the instrument in the chapel of Concordia College in Oakland, California.[73] Rodney Gehrke, Hugo's son, also commented,

> He designed the first modern tracker organ in California (if not the whole west coast) at Peace Lutheran Church, Mill Valley, just north of the Golden Gate Bridge in 1959 and designed dozens of other organs for (mostly) Lutheran churches, including, of course, the organ at Concordia, Milwaukee.[74]

Gehrke also felt that "the organ should be, first and foremost, an enabler of congregational and choral music rather than 'just' a performance instrument."[75] Rodney Gehrke further commented that this instrument, built by Werner Bosch Organ Company of Kassel, Germany, for Concordia College, Milwaukee, was one of his father's favorite instruments.

In the January 17, 1962 edition of the *Concordia Courier*, the college announced that a new organ would be built and installed in the chapel. The old Wangerin organ was "enclosed in a chamber" and had been in use in the chapel for 15 years.[76] Glenn Mahnke, a Concordia student during that time, recalls that the old organ chamber was located "immediately behind the chancel/altar" and served as a storage closet after the old organ had been decommissioned."[77] It was a small organ that spoke into the nave of the chapel from a small room. It can safely be said that this was not an ideal organ installation.

In contrast, the new organ had exposed Great and Pedal divisions and was to be approximately twice the size of the old instrument. "Engel stated that, when the pipes are exposed, they carry a crisper, clearer, and brighter tone than when enclosed." He also stated "the new organ will give us an opportunity here at this school to hear the music of our Lutheran heritage as it was originally intended to be heard."[78] The organ was to be placed along the back wall of the chapel on the central axis of the nave.

According to the September 28, 1962 issue of the *Concordia Courier*, Werner Bosch came over to the United States to talk with Engel and see the space where his instrument would be installed. They discussed "plans for remodeling the chapel chancel to permit proper placing of the organ and its 1,800 pipes."[79] This meeting took place on September 19, 1962. (See Appendix C—Concordia Chapel to get new organ.)

"The organ, of classical or baroque design, is being built by the Werner Bosch Organ Company of Kassel, New Frankfurt, in Hesse, Germany"[80] The organ was designed as a mechanical (tracker) action instrument, one of the first in the upper Midwest during the 1960s. A mechanical/tracker action instrument provides the organist with a direct physical link from the keys to the pipes via a system of levers. As Engel said at that time, "The Concordia organ will be the only one of its kind in the Midwest."[81] Since then, the German tracker-action organ seems more commonplace, but at that time, Concordia College was on the cutting edge of the organ revival movement.

At the time of the order, Bosch commented that while European builders preferred to use time-honored techniques in their organ building (such as tracker action and slider chests), they realized that organists also wished to play modern works. The organ must accommodate that music as well as the traditional musical styles.

There is great value to the use of classic building techniques, including "clean tone and clarity of line." "We have an assignment that urges us to be alert to contemporary developments and to address ourselves to the possibilities of our own day."[82] James Burmeister, former music minister at Memorial Lutheran Church in Glendale, Wisconsin indicated that he has seen the original plans for the organ. The console was intended to have draw-knobs on either side of the key-desk and that it would be an integral part of the case in the tradition of European organs. However, it was later decided that the console, while attached, would "be more American." Thus the console of the instrument was constructed complete with rocker tabs, a roll top cover and was, while still attached, slightly away from the main case of the organ.[83]

> The entire organ is in an oak case with its wood originating in the southern forest area of Germany. The instrument consists of twenty-seven stops (thirty-three ranks) and has mechanical action. The keyboards have ebony natural keys with the sharps being made of pear wood with ivory overlays. The pedal natural keys are made of maple with ebony sharps. The pipes of the organ are made of lead, tin or zinc with the wood pipes of oak or mahogany. Atop the twenty-one foot-high case containing 1668 pipes is a Zimbelstern.[84]

The organ was installed in the fall of 1963. Mrs. Engel commented that Engel was very excited about the arrival of this new instrument. Mahnke recalls that "when the Bosch organ was installed, Engel was constantly arm-twisting students to carry pipe crates and other organ parts up to the second floor chapel."

> Jim was like the proverbial "kid in a candy shop" and spent hours assisting or simply nosing around as the organ was

erected in the rear of the chapel. Jim took all the shipping container wood to his home and paneled his basement with it, proudly displaying all the stamps from shipping![85]

Bosch did all the preliminary voicing for the Concordia instrument in his shop in Germany and then traveled over to the United States to personally finish voicing and tuning it. When he was done, this instrument had the sound that Bosch intended it to have and served as a prime example of his work.

Concordia College held the organ dedication service on November 17, 1963. About 400 people attended the dedication service and President Walter Stuenkel preached the dedicatory sermon. Engel played for the dedication service "and directed choirs of the college and high school departments."[86] (See Appendix A—Engel at the console of the chapel organ.)

Hugo Gehrke presented a dedicatory recital on January 12, 1964, to a "more than capacity crowd."[87] Many of the well-known Lutheran organ composers of the time were represented in the program including the works of Bender, Manz, and Engel. Mahnke commented that he vividly recalled attending Gehrke's recital and that it was so well attended that there was "standing room only" in the chapel.[88] These two dedicatory gatherings were indeed landmark events for Concordia College and its music department. (See Appendix C—photo and specification of the organ in the chapel.)

This organ was in service at the Concordia College Chapel until the college moved to its new Mequon campus in 1983. A benefit recital and hymn sing was held on Sunday, June 26, 1983. A number of local Milwaukee organists played sections of the program. This was the last major recital event that was held on the old Concordia campus with this organ.

Concordia College sold the Bosch organ to Memorial Lutheran Church in Glendale, Wisconsin, a northern suburb of Milwaukee. It was dismantled and kept in storage until the church's sanctuary was ready to house it. Burmeister, who was the music director at Memorial Lutheran Church, explained how the organ has changed through the years since it left Concordia's chapel. When the organ was reassembled, they replaced the metal trackers with wooden ones and felted the stop motors when it was reassembled at Memorial Lutheran Church. The act of adding felt to the stop motors made the organ action a little quieter. He also told me that the tracker (mechanical) action was adjusted so that the organ was easier to play. The organ keys were previously stiff and hard to play.[89] The author had the opportunity to play the instrument and found the current action to be light and responsive.

This was one of the first organs by Bosch to be imported. There is a lot of nicking on the pipes so that the sound of the instrument is smooth. There is not that overabundance of chiff that a person might expect to hear from many organs built and voiced during that time period. Burmeister explained that later Bosch organs were shipped over here unvoiced. Bosch had set the example and his thought was that a local voicer from the United States would finish voicing the organ in his style. In certain cases, the organs were not voiced to Bosch's specifications. Unfortunately, those organs were harsher and more percussive than he had actually intended them to be.[90] (For pictures and further information about this organ, see Appendix C—Bosch organ at Memorial Lutheran Church.)

When Mahnke started attending Concordia, Milwaukee in 1964, the student body was increasing as was Engel's teaching load. Two other professors were called in to teach music part-time in order to assist Engel. These professors were Loren O. Barker and Arno Klausmeier.

Professor Barker "directed the band and gave some instrumental music lessons."[91] Rev. Professor Klausmeier was new to the faculty that year and it was anticipated that he would take over the choral duties in order to free up some of Engel's time. Circumstances changed near the end of October and Engel again took up the baton to direct the choir. The choir practiced in earnest, but there wasn't enough time to present a proper Christmas Concert that year. However, a concert "was performed in January 1965 to a packed audience in the college gymnasium."[92]

An interesting story that Glenn Mahnke relayed revolves around a college choir tour that occurred in the spring of 1965. Choir tours can be fun, exciting, tiring and stressful. In the case of this recollection they were more tiring and stressful than fun and exciting.

Our tour in spring, 1965 was Iowa and Wisconsin. One evening, we sang in Marcus, Iowa, in the northwestern part of the state. The next evening, we were slated to sing at Zion Lutheran Church, Wausau, WI. Since there is no *good* direct route...and the bus was faster *without* the air-conditioning running, we left Marcus, Iowa at 3:30am, and made it to Wausau in time for dinner before the concert. Whew! Great planning, Jim![93]

During the fall semester of 1965, the first female students were admitted into Concordia College. The institution was now a coeducational junior college with the ability to grant Associate of Arts degrees to both men and women. Professor Eldon Balko, who was a professor at Concordia College at that time, commented that teacher education students would get their associate's degree and then finish with their bachelor's degree at Concordia, River Forest, Concordia, Seward, Nebraska, or at Concordia in St. Paul.[94]

The transition to a co-ed institution caused major changes to the faculty, curriculum and the college facilities.

Change is never easy and adjustment takes time. This was true with the addition of women to the student body. Throughout the history of Concordia College through the spring semester of 1965, the student body at the college was exclusively male. One might call it a "brotherhood." Now there were women on campus and some of the male students were not exactly happy about it at first. Mahnke recalls those days:

> I was a sophomore in college when the first women were admitted. My class included two: Ethel Rupprecht [Oliver Rupprecht's daughter] and Gloria Muellenbach-Tonn. All the other women were admitted to the freshman class. Many of us six-year men looked down on this and frowned for about two days. Then, we quickly came to the conclusion that girls were good![95]

Balko, in an effort to make the transition smoother, decided to keep the College and High School male choruses going, but also added a mixed choir to the curriculum to include the women. He recalls that the first class including young ladies was small, which was to be expected at the beginning. Female voices were at a premium and due to this fact, Balko required all women in the freshman class to audition for the choir. "If I felt they had sufficient talent, 'Chamber Singers' appeared on their schedule of classes. Some made efforts to appeal the decision, but my answer was always, 'conducting is the last of the great dictatorships; therefore, your request is denied.'"[96]

With this major change and an enrollment of over 600 students at that time, there came a need for more music faculty. In the 1965-66 school year, Concordia College saw its first mixed college choir, directed by Balko. As he put it: "I came in with the girls."[97] He was called to Concordia College to take over the direction of the choirs, which he did until he left Concordia College to teach at the University of Wisconsin—Milwaukee in 1975. Engel focused on classroom teaching and organ instruction during this time period. Balko says the following regarding the curriculum at Concordia during 1965-1969:

> The music curriculum included academic courses that are usual in the first two years of any college music education: Elementary Theory, Music Appreciation, major instrument requirements, ensemble requirements. Opportunities for electives were minimal. I do believe Jim offered an elementary composition class and I offered an introduction to conducting. As you know, the course work during the first couple of years of secondary education is principally general requirements. Ensemble offerings included Chamber Singers, Chapel Singers, High School Male Chorus, and Band. Private instruction was offered in voice, piano, and organ. The only extracurricular offering that I recall was the "Chorale Club" led by Professor Oliver Rupprecht.[98]

A new classroom building was added that same year.[99] As noted in the *Concordia College Centennial Jubilee:1881-1981*, this was the last building that was built on the Concordia's Milwaukee campus before the move to Mequon in 1983. In the late 1960s, Concordia decided to phase out its high school department due to declining enrollments. The process of phasing out this department began in the 1970-1971 school year and was completed in 1973.[100] Those were just some of the changes that occurred while Engel served at Concordia.

With all of these changes that took place during this time, the author had to ask the question: What were students like at Concordia during this period of time? This was the 1960s, when the Vietnam conflict was at the forefront of students' lives. Social strife was gripping many major metropolitan areas across the United States, including Milwaukee. Student activism was running high on many college campuses. Some of that activism ended up becoming full-blown campus riots as what happened at Kent State University and a few other major colleges and universities. One might think that these issues and trends would have affected the student body at Concordia College, but that was not the case. Balko said it best when he relayed the following:

> Yet, the kids who enrolled at Concordia were different. Their foremost purpose at this point in their lives was to get an education. Their maturity gave evidence of their Christian upbringing. They were aware of the turmoil occurring on other campuses, of the student marches throughout major metropolitan cities, of the physical destruction that was rampant, etc., but they limited their participation to constructive discussion. They were amazing young people whom, had they been noticed, could have played a major role in the healing process.[101]

These were the type of students whom Engel taught at Concordia. Many of them became leaders in the Lutheran Church—Missouri Synod: pastors, teachers and laypeople.

While at Concordia, the Engels invited students over on occasion. Geis recalled that this was during the time when the college only enrolled male students. Engel would "invite some of his older students over for a game or two of cards."[102]

Mahnke recalls visiting the Engel's home on a number of occasions. The first vignette is about the Engel's patio and how they tried to personalize it in a unique fashion.

> Jim and Norma decided to "dress-up" their patio by putting down cement "paver-blocks." Jim, always the musician, decided to do it in two colors and make a giant treble clef with the blocks. Well, he *did* get it done, but

the only place you could really see it and understand it was from the *roof of the house.*[103]

The second anecdote revolves around a card game known as Sheepshead. In the German, it is called *Schafskopf.* It is a game that has been played since the time of J. S. Bach and is still played by German Americans to this day.

> Jim loved to play [Sheepshead] and would often invite college students to his home on Friday, Saturday or Sunday evenings to play, eat snacks, and have a great time. Jim wasn't the sharpest Sheepshead player, but we did have fun.[104]

Mahnke also recalls that Engel's grand piano sat in the dining room. Engel used to place his cello under the piano when he was not practicing it. "The entire time I knew him, he was attempting to teach himself how to play the cello! I don't think he ever did learn how![105]

Geis recalls how much her parents enjoyed having students over on those evenings. "One very special student, Ben Asen, visited often and even stayed with us over a summer. It was like having a big brother in the house." Geis said that her father was always concerned about his students and went out of his way to help them. "Dad really wanted his students to do well in school.[106] The praise that his former students have lavished on him, along with their accomplishments, is proof of this fact.

During the last few years at Concordia, Engel became more and more concerned about the direction that the Lutheran Church—Missouri Synod was headed doctrinally. Engel was a conservative, confessional Lutheran and did not agree with some of the things he saw happening in his church body. There were many changes going on, along with growing conflict and division. Balko commented that these divisions and conflicts within the LCMS deeply hurt Engel.[107]

Mahnke recalls:

> I do recall standing in the parking lot surrounded by the gym, the old classroom building and the administration building, having a discussion with Jim not too long before he left the college. He cautioned me about the theology of some [at Concordia Teachers College, River Forest,

Illinois], but I mentioned to him that the vast majority of my theology credits came from Milwaukee. He was pleased with that.[108]

Engel ultimately severed ties with his beloved LCMS in 1972 and joined the Wisconsin Evangelical Lutheran Synod.

The old Concordia campus still physically exists in the heart of Milwaukee. It was sold to the Indian Community School of Milwaukee in 1986 and is currently owned and operated by them. It consists of eleven acres and seven major buildings, same as it did when Engel taught there. While Engel taught at Concordia College, Geis recalled that the Engel family lived in a "small three-bedroom bungalow in a modest, middle class neighborhood of Milwaukee." It was a two-story house with bedrooms on the second story. There are many such middle class neighborhoods in Milwaukee. Unlike suburban living today, the houses in such neighborhoods were often quite close together with compact lots. They had a small back yard that included a small patio and picnic table. There was not a lot of room where the children could play. Geis commented that the Engel family had a "golden retriever named Ginger." They had a television set, but it only could pick up three channels. Beyond that they had a ping-pong table in the basement. "Our garage was filled with old bikes and tools." The "dining room" was the centerpiece of the house, not because it contained a fine dining room table, but rather because it served as the music room. In the "dining room" one would find a fine grand piano, his prized harpsichord and a picture of Bach on the wall. Beyond that, the Engel family enjoyed a normal family life, typical for people living in the city of Milwaukee in the 1950s and 1960s. "We ate supper together, cut our own grass and shoveled our own snow. We had our share of unusual neighbors and lots of visits from friends and relatives."[109]

Engel dearly loved his mother. Geis recalls that her grandmother's house was relatively close to the Concordia College campus. During the school year, Engel would make a point of going over to his mother's house for lunch. It was a time for good food and good conversation. Geis recalls that her grandmother was "gentle and kind" and that she "lived well into old age."[110]

Musical Service at Gospel Lutheran Church, Milwaukee

Engel was also active in the music ministry of Gospel Evangelical Lutheran Church, located in Milwaukee at the corner of 16th Street and Capitol Drive. (See Appendix B—Gospel Evangelical Lutheran Church.) According to Gospel Lutheran's 80th anniversary booklet, he began his work as the organist and choir director on September 15, 1957. The author had the privilege of talking with Mrs. Dorothy Piel, who has been a friend of the Engel family since they were members at Gospel Lutheran and sang in his church choir since he started directing it. The membership in the Gospel Choir averaged between forty-two and forty-six members. Piel commented that his was the best choir in which she had the opportunity to sing. During this time, Engel directed the Gospel Choir in works such as selections from *Messiah* by G. F. Handel. "The music that he taught us to sing in church is rarely done by church choirs."[111] Another interesting note was that Piel's husband had perfect pitch. Geis recalls that her dad would often ask him to supply the pitch when they sang a cappella. Mr. Piel would hum the note and then they would sing.

The Gospel Lutheran Choir also occasionally sang outside the congregation. He took his church choir to sing for a Concordia chapel service on one occasion. Piel recalls being inspired by all of the men singing the hymns in the service. The Gospel Choir also sang at the 100th anniversary of Immanuel Lutheran Church in Milwaukee, located on the southwest corner of Teutonia and Meinecke. They, along with the Immanuel Church Choir, sang a "Festival of Song" service on October 2, 1966. The choral concert was very well received by Immanuel congregation.[112]

As a special treat for the Gospel Choir at Christmastime, Professor and Mrs. Engel would invite the choir over to their house for a "Trim-the-Tree Christmas Party." Geis vividly recalls these yearly events:

> We children were not permitted to attend this party; however, we would sit on the stairs that led up to our second story bedrooms and wait for individual choir members to open the door and pass us cookies and cake and sometimes entire plates of food! My father had a terrific sense of humor, as did many of the members of his choir. The

sound of song and laughter would fill the house until the wee hours of the morning.[113]

Geis commented that she had good memories surrounding Gospel Lutheran Church. A number of these revolve around her father and the organ at Gospel. Her father would periodically take her along to help him tune the pipe organ. Since the pipes were in front and the console was in the balcony, Engel needed help. "I would sit on the organ bench in the balcony, he would show me which keys to press, and then he would go up to the front of the church and climb into the pipes. The church was dark and shadowy. I would be a little afraid but then my father's voice would bellow out from behind the altar. "Up one", he would say, or "down one." I would go up and down the keyboard until the job was done and we were on our way home again."[114] Engel's daughter, Joan, also recalls helping her father tune the Gospel organ by being a key holder.

When Engel came to serve Gospel Lutheran Church, they were worshiping in the present building. A Wangerin Organ (Opus 760) was installed at the time of the sanctuary's dedication in 1939. The pipework was located in a chamber above the sacristy, located on the left side of the chancel. At the time that Engel served this congregation, the organ console was located in the balcony.[115]

The author had the opportunity to correspond with Stanton Peters, a leading pipe organ tonal director and former president of the Schlicker Organ Company of Buffalo, New York. As Peters pointed out, the original location of the organ pipework was consistent with a movement in the Lutheran church that started during the 1920s where choirs were moved from the balcony to the front of the church. Small transepts were designed for them and the organ console was often placed in that alcove. "Many, many churches, not only here but all over the country, were designed with choir areas off to one side to the Chancel."[116] The pipes were often placed in a chamber above the sacristy with an opening into the chancel space. The sound of the organ bounced off the opposite wall of the chancel and spilled out into the nave. Considering that the pipes were way above and across from the singers, and the fact that the singers were in a transept, the cohesion of sound and proper projection into the nave were nearly impossible.

Since the console of the Gospel organ was located in the balcony during Engel's early tenure at Gospel Lutheran, the situation was even less ideal than it would have been if the whole instrument had been located in the front of the church. Due to the time it took for an electrical signal to travel from the balcony to the pipework up front, there would have been a speech delay between the playing of a note at a console and the sound coming from the pipe. Additionally, there is the acoustical delay for that sound to make it back to the organist's ears. This would not be an ideal situation for coordinating the organ with the choir and other instruments located in the balcony. Being a promoter of the "Organ Reform Movement"[117] and a former student of Gehrke, Engel would have seen the disadvantages of that configuration and would have desired to correct those deficiencies.

> I think Engel was very aware of these drawbacks and want-
> ed to set an example for other churches to both restore
> the organ to the rear gallery position as well as provide
> the proper tonal resources for congregational singing,
> choir accompaniment and the music of the liturgy.[118]

With this consideration, in 1962 the congregation authorized the spending of $12,000 to enlarge, renovate and move the organ pipes from the chancel chamber to the balcony. The organ was re-built and completely moved into the balcony by Otto Eberle, the same man who helped with the Bosch organ at Concordia. From what Mr. Peters recalled when he worked on the organ in the years after 1974, the Swell 8' Salicional, 8' Voix Celeste, 4' Flute and Pedal 16' Bourdon were from the original Wangerin instrument. Peters recalls that Otto Eberle purchased all of the new ranks from the Werner Bosch Organ Company. The console was also re-built at that time "with a new combination action from Klann."[119] According to Peters, Eberle, Bosch and Herman Schlicker apprenticed at the Steinmeyer organ firm in Oettingen, Germany.[120] Due to Eberle's voicing, the organ at Gospel has a light, crisp sound similar to many other neo-baroque organs built during the late 1960s.

Of course, the influence of Engel cannot be denied. While he was not directly involved in the design of the Bosch organ at Concordia, he certainly was influenced by it. It is the author's contention that Engel, as well as the balcony placement of the Gospel organ, heavily influenced the tonal design of the Gospel organ. "It would also be logical that in addition to a more modern specification and voicing, Jim Engel would desire a far better physical placement (the rear gallery) so that the instrument would better project to the congregation."[121] The organ, in its current form and location, speaks directly and effortlessly down the nave. The choir area, now located in the balcony, is on the same level as the organ, and coordination between these musical forces is now easy. While Stanton Peters did not know Engel well, he had the opportunity to talk with him on a number of occasions regarding organ design and construction. "I had the great pleasure of meeting Engel on a number of occasions in the late 1970s and it was always clear to me that he was quite progressive in his thoughts on organ building, placement and tonal design. In this area of the country he was one of the leading proponents of what has now become known as the Organ Reform Movement."[122] (For further information about the organ, see Appendix C—photos and specification of the Gospel organ.)

The dedication of the new Gospel Lutheran organ took place on September 8, 1968, at 7:30 p.m. The program incorporated the organ, the Gospel Choir and the Concordia College Brass Ensemble. Engel was the organist for the occasion. (For a list of the works included in this program, see Appendix C—Bulletin from the Organ Dedication at Gospel Lutheran Church.)

One of the most tragic events in the history of Gospel Lutheran Church was the church fire, which occurred on December 5, 1971. Jeffrey Hammes, former co-owner of Hammes/Foxe Organ Company and an organ student of Engel, recalls that evening:

> I do remember the evening of the fire which happened to be when Mt Calvary was having its final Christmas concert rehearsal and Engel was the organist. He came running in for the rehearsal, telling us that his church was on fire and he was most concerned about losing his music.[123]

Mary Geis commented about her father's feelings about this tragedy. While the condition of the church's choral music was very important to him, the thought that the house of the Lord was on fire was devastating. It was heartbreaking for him to see this place of prayer and worship destroyed—a place where he and his family had worshiped for many years.[124] One can imagine the sadness of the congregation since this fire devastated the church building right before Christmas. To make matters worse, the fire was caused by an arsonist. The fire damaged the chancel area of the church, and there was smoke damage throughout the sanctuary. Piel commented that the church was under repair for three months. The sanctuary was re-dedicatated on March 19th, 1972 at both the 8:00 a.m. and 10:30 a.m. services. Since this was still Lent, the congregation was able to celebrate Palm Sunday and Easter in their church building.[125]

The aftermath of the fire brought the choir together to reclaim the church's burned choral music and raise money for new choir robes. Piel recalls these events. "We all worked together to get our choir room and all the music separated from too badly burned to just a little burned and tried to save most of the copies or purchase extra copies. We paid to replace our choir robes and never had asked the church for one penny to replace or to buy robes or music even before the fire."[126] The choir worked hard to get everything cleaned up and reorganized, but it also had the effect of making them a close-knit group. "The fire on December 5, 1971, brought the choir members together as not just friends but like we were a family."[127]

In the late spring of 1972, the Engels prepared to move to Appleton. Piel mentioned that Gospel's church choir had a farewell party for them on June 17, 1972. It was during that same month that the family moved to Appleton so that Engel could assume his new duties at Fox Valley Lutheran High School in Appleton, Wisconsin.[128]

Other Musical Activities in the Milwaukee Area and Missouri Synod

Besides serving at Concordia College in Milwaukee and Gospel Lutheran Church, Engel took a keen interest in the state of music in the Missouri Synod. Arthur Preuss from St. John Lutheran Church in Racine commented that in 1960 he served with Engel on a committee which was charged with the task of "encouraging people to go into church work." This committee consisted of three members and the third member of this team was Harold Albers, teacher and director of music at Our Redeemer Lutheran Church and School, Wauwatosa,

Wisconsin. The members of this committee traveled around to various churches and schools in the LCMS in order to promote the value of music in worship and the need for workers in this field.[129] Engel's activity within the Missouri Synod foreshadowed some of his later interest and work in promoting quality church music and musicianship within the Wisconsin Synod.

Engel was well known in the Milwaukee area as an excellent recitalist and musician. During his residency in Milwaukee, he served as a recitalist at a number of churches. Dr. Edward Meyer, professor emeritus from Dr. Martin Luther College, New Ulm, MN, commented that he heard Engel on a number of occasions. He heard Engel play on the Bosch at Concordia, a recital at Cross Lutheran Church and at Gospel Lutheran Church.[130] Mrs. Engel commented that Engel "also had the opportunity to play at the Marcus Center for the Performing Arts for joint Reformation services when he lived in Milwaukee."[131] (The Marcus Center was once known as the Milwaukee Performing Arts Center or PAC.) Uihlein Hall, the main concert hall at the Marcus Center, houses a three-manual Aeolian Skinner concert pipe organ. Craig Hirschman recalls that only certain people with special credentials and permission were allowed to play that organ and Engel was one of these people. Mahnke also recalled seeing him play this instrument.

> While I don't recall what music was performed, I vividly recall Jim playing a major Bach prelude and fugue on the Aeolian-Skinner organ in Uihlein Hall. I do recall that Jim, ever the modest musician, had difficulty accepting the resounding applause given him by the full house.[132]

During the time he taught at Concordia, Engel began to pursue his doctorate at the University of Wisconsin in Madison. He took coursework during the summers of 1962-1964 and whenever he could in subsequent years. While he went to school full time, he was a teaching assistant and stayed at the LCMS Chapel in Madison. Mrs. Engel said that the chapel had "sleeping rooms and a kitchen. His duties (while staying at the chapel) were to unlock the chapel doors in the morning and lock them up in the evening."[133] Between 1969 and 1971, Engel was able to get a sabbatical to finish his doctoral coursework. During this time, he co-authored a curriculum with

Bruce Benward entitled *Beginning Music Theory: A High School Credit Course*. A copy of this two-volume work resides in a library at the University of Wisconsin in Madison. He finished his coursework in 1971 but did not complete his dissertation.

Teaching at Fox Valley Lutheran High School, Appleton

The year 1972 was a year of great change for the Engel family. After joining the Wisconsin Evangelical Synod, Engel accepted a call to teach at Fox Valley Lutheran High School in Appleton.

Fox Valley Lutheran High School was founded by the Wisconsin Evangelical Lutheran Synod in 1953. When Engel accepted the call to serve the school, the campus was located at 2626 North Oneida Street in Appleton and had recently gone through an expansion phase. (See Appendix B—Fox Valley Lutheran High School.)

Music rooms, along with many other teaching spaces, had been added during the 1964-65 school year. During the early 1970s when Engel taught there, the school had between 500 and 600 students. The building, which was designed for 500 students, had become overcrowded and in need of yet another expansion. This necessary expansion took place just after Engel accepted the call to teach at Dr. Martin Luther College, New Ulm, MN in 1975.[134]

Engel's primary duties at Fox Valley Lutheran High School were to teach mathematics and the high school choirs. Mrs. Engel commented that he found teaching at the high school level to be a real adjustment after teaching at the college level for so many years.[135] Dr. Edward Meyer, retired professor from Dr. Martin Luther College, commented that he first met Engel, Engel was still a teacher at Fox Valley Lutheran. Engel was attending a conference which was being held on the Dr. Martin Luther College campus. Meyer saw that he was eating alone and decided to join him for lunch. Engel commented to Meyer that he found teaching high school students a real challenge. In response to the high demands of Engel's position, he focused his energies into teaching his students and they benefited from his efforts.[136]

While Fox Valley Lutheran already had a music program, it began to flower under Engel's leadership. Brenda Glodowski, who had

Engel for her junior and senior years, recalls what the music program was like before Engel came to Fox Valley Lutheran.

> When I was a freshman at Fox Valley Lutheran High School, there was no such thing as a freshman choir. We sat through a hymnology course. It was very dry and boring. The class could have been an interesting class if we could have sung hymns. I kept thinking: "Man, can't we sing? I want to sing." And so, because there was no freshman choir, I could hardly wait to become a sophomore so I could join the choir. Everyone was in that choir—sophomores, juniors, and seniors. There was only one choir. During the freshman hymnology course, the boys were misbehaving. The teacher didn't have good control, and it wasn't a very good experience.[137]

Engel started a number of new groups and collaborated to offer other worthwhile experiences for his students. He started the Fox Valley Lutheran High School Choraliers, a freshman choir, and other choirs. Glodowski tells us about those times and her experiences.

> But then Mr. Engel came and started turning things around. As I looked through my high school yearbooks, there were pictures of only one choir for each year, except my senior year. All of a sudden there was a freshman choir, and then there's the concert choir and then there was this choir called "Seventh Hour Choir," meaning we met during the seventh hour of the day. I don't remember how it happened but it wound up being the group that went to Choral Festival. I would have never had that experience if he had not made that happen. I remember that choral festival was just amazing to me. And now I am taking kids to Choral Festival from West Lutheran High School where I teach. I just think back to those days when I cried at those choral festivals and now my kids are crying at the choral festival just because it's such a moving experience. I only got to go to a choral festival once.
>
> I also remember that experience because he let me help pick out the outfits and allowed me to do the choreog-

raphy. He really gave me many wonderful opportunities with that experience. I think he really started a lot of choral groups at the high school when he was there. He gave many students opportunities that they would normally not have had.[138]

Mrs. Engel commented on the first Christmas concert at Fox Valley Lutheran High School.

The first Christmas Concert—with silhouettes. The idea of silhouettes is to surround the audience with singers and fill the concert space with sound. The director stands in one central spot and directs everyone. The choir members have to watch carefully in order for the choir to be synchronized. The effect is impressive but also hard to coordinate. The choir marched in from the sides and the people said, "We have a musician here now. . . . The people were all amazed.[139]

Engel's daughter, Joan Mueller, commented that "he did the whole thing and always with grace and elegance."[140] Mrs. Engel added, "And humility."[141] Mueller further commented that "What Dad did, Dad did well. And he always said, 'If you are going to do it, do it well.'"[142]

Engel also worked closely with the drama department to put on full-scale musicals. He collaborated with David Pelzl and Eugene Baer to create Fox Valley Lutheran's first full-scale musical. The title of that first musical was *Ask Any Girl*. Mrs. Engel and Mueller recalled that Engel played the full score on piano for the musical practices. He also performed that first musical on the piano along with two violins, a viola and a cello. For subsequent musicals, he hired an orchestra from Lawrence University. The second musical was *The Sound of Music*. Glodowski recalls that this "was a huge big deal because it was the first time we ever did a big main musical at Fox Valley." He "helped prepare the chorus, and he worked with the soloists for the musicals both years."[143] He also allowed Glodowski to help him with the music for the musicals. Geis recalls that her sister, Joan, had the starring role in one of these high school musicals. "One of the highlights of this time period was a high school play in which my sister, Joan, had the leading female part and Dad was the director! Joan had a beautiful voice."[144] This most certainly was a time of pride and joy for the Engel family.

Other Musical Activities While Living in Appleton

In 1973 Engel became the director of the Valley Lutheran Chorale in Appleton.[145] It was a choir for adult members of local WELS congregations and was similar in scope to the Lutheran A Cappella Choir in Milwaukee which Hugo Gehrke directed. Mrs. Engel commented that, during the time her husband was the director, the Chorale sang a couple major concerts each year.[146] After the Engels left Appleton, the Valley Lutheran Chorale continued to perform under a new director. While living in Appleton, Engel regularly served as an organist at St. Peter Evangelical Lutheran Church, located in Freedom, Wisconsin on the northeast edge of Appleton. (See Appendix B—St. Peter Lutheran Church.) Pastor Ash, one of the pastors at St. Peter's, accepted a call to the church in 1974. When he came to the church, he found that there was a shortage of organists at this congregation. Consequently, Engel was playing at St. Peter Lutheran on a regular basis. Ash recalls that he only played the organ at the church and nothing more.[147]

The present church was completed and dedicated in December of 1907 and was built on the foundation of the previous church that had burned down that previous May. The previous church building had included a 1903, seven-stop, organ which was built by the George Weickhardt Organ Company of Milwaukee, Wisconsin. A nearly identical instrument was installed in the new church in 1907.[148] This organ has been in service for over 100 years and is currently in operational condition. It was renovated within the last decade. The repairs included a cleaning and refurbishing of the chestwork, solid-state key action and a new set of chimes.[149] The chimes have their own mini-keyboard. The current instrument, as it exists in 2007, consists of six ranks, one manual, and pedal. Beyond these repairs, Engel would still recognize today's instrument as the one he played back in the early-mid 1970s. (See Appendix C— Weickhardt Organ.)

During his years in Appleton, Engel played a number of organ dedication recitals throughout the Fox Valley region. One of these recitals was at the dedication of the pipe organ at St. Matthew Lutheran Church in Appleton. He also played for the dedication of a number of electronic organs in the region. Engel also gave a number of organ concerts for Schultz Music Store, Appleton, Wisconsin. Mrs. Engel also said that her husband played for a WELS National Choral Festival, which was held at the Marcus Center for the Performing Arts in Milwaukee during his three years in Appleton, Wisconsin.[150] The author recalls hearing about these national choral events held in Milwaukee when he was a child.

Engel owned a couple of electronic organs through his life so that he would be able to practice and later teach lessons from home. He purchased his first instrument while the Engels lived in Milwaukee. It was a used practice organ from Alverno College in Milwaukee. This instrument served him for some time while he lived in Milwaukee and later in Appleton.[151] While the author does not know what this instrument was like, the technology of the time focused on the use of vacuum tubes—the same technology that one could find in televisions of that period. When the instrument was "warmed up," the tubes that produced the sound for the organ would glow. They had a warm, full sound, but most people would not confuse their sound with that of a pipe organ. Near the end of his time living in Appleton, he was able to purchase a two-manual Allen electronic organ with full pedal board. Mrs. Engel commented that he gave lessons at home on that instrument. She said that he was very excited about having that instrument, especially due to the rarity of having such an instrument at home.[152] Mueller recalled that her father used to practice in the middle of the night with the volume down low when he was nervous, preparing for a big concert or a recital.[153] This instrument moved with the family too until it was donated to Messiah Lutheran Church, a small congregation in Forest Lake, MN.[154]

Engel also knew how to play the harpsichord. Mrs. Engel relayed that he built a harpsichord from a kit while he was a professor at Concordia College, Milwaukee. One of his brothers, who was gifted in the area of woodworking, built a cherry wood case for the instrument. Engel used his harpsichord at times to accompany the Concordia choir. Later, he took his harpsichord on DMLC choir tours.[155]

Teaching at Dr. Martin Luther College, New Ulm.

In 1975, Engel received and accepted a call to serve as a music professor at Dr. Martin Luther College in New Ulm, MN. Geis commented that her father was happy to be teaching college level students again.[156] According to Meyer, there was a need for teachers of music theory at the time and Engel first taught the freshman theory classes. At the time, the course title for this class was "Basic Musicianship." "It was a one-year course that involved sight singing and music reading, as well as basic music knowledge."[157] Meyer also pointed out that while there was a basic curriculum for "Basic Musicianship," each of the classes was taught at varied skill levels depending on the background skill of the incoming freshman. Those students who came in with little background were placed in basic classes, while students who already had a music background in high school were placed into more challenging classes. Students who had taken piano, organ, choir and music theory/appreciation classes were good candidates for the advanced freshman coursework. "We probably had as many as four to five different levels."[158] Engel taught all of the different "Basic Musicianship" course levels during his tenure at Dr. Martin Luther College (DMLC) but later gravitated toward teaching the more advanced freshman students.

Over time, he started teaching upper level music theory and composition. Since he was a composer, teaching such classes was a good fit for him. "He and Waldemar Nolte alternated one year. Professor Nolte would have the upper theory classes and then the next year he would have them."[159]

One of the capstone classes that Engel developed and taught was "Counterpoint for Parish Musicians." This course taught the student how to compose counterpoint that would be useful in a parish situation. (The author has taken a similar course while earning his undergraduate degree and found it to be rewarding, both from a general understanding standpoint, as well as from a compositional standpoint.) It is important to note that in addition to developing the curriculum for this course, Engel developed his own textbook, which he used with his students. He did this because there was not a textbook on the market at that time which covered the material in the fashion that Engel wished to cover it. (The author has seen a copy of this textbook and was impressed by the scope and content of the material which Engel used.) Craig Hirschmann, a former student at Dr. Martin Luther College, commented that Engel's text truly had the scope of a conventional published textbook. "He wrote a preface and he gave us the whole thing as notes in his own hand. It's the whole course and we didn't make it completely through the course, so you'll see blank pages."[160] The students unfortunately did not complete as much of the coursework as Engel would have liked at the time when Hirschmann took the course He also remembers that Engel would write course packs for other courses that he taught as well. As a supplement to his manuals and course packs, Engel would direct his students to consult Walter Piston's *Harmony*.[161] Meyer commented that the counterpoint course was "quite successful."[162] Meyer continued to teach the course after Engel's death for about four semesters. This course is no longer part of the college's current music curriculum.

Another key responsibility for Engel was teaching organ lessons. During his first semester at DMLC, he instructed seventeen organ students.[163] He taught all levels of organ students, from beginners to advanced learners. Meyer commented that organ students were assigned to the organ professors by the organ committee chairman. A professor could not dictate that he or she wanted only advanced students or beginning students. It was the chairman who made the decision on which professor an incoming student was assigned to and not the individual organ teacher or the organ student. Dr. Bruce Backer was the organ committee chairman during the Engel's tenure at DMLC and made those decisions for many years. "Like the rest of us, we simply were assigned students." However, on occasion, an incoming student might make a request for a specific professor. Such requests would be considered by the organ committee chairman and occasionally granted. "Otherwise, Engel was given the students as they came. There was no preference made."[164]

Hirschmann was one of those students for which an exception was made. He entered DMLC as a freshman in the fall of 1980 and had Engel as his organ instructor for all four years. Hirschmann recalls that Engel often seemed to have more of the gifted players. While Hirschmann attended there, Engel seemed to have very few freshmen studying organ with him. At the urging of Elizabeth Wessel, who was a senior at DMLC at that time, Hirschmann recalls writing to the DMLC music department requesting Engel before he arrived for classes. When Hirschmann did arrive on campus, Engel said, "'I don't have room for you, except I have this one time,' and it was my lunch hour."[165] This was a real problem since Hirschmann had a class before and after his lunch period. He was so motivated to study with Engel that he willingly skipped lunch. This continued for over a month before Engel became aware of the situation and switched Hirschmann's lesson to another time.[166]

As Engel had done so often in his past teaching posts, he directed choirs at DMLC. One of the choirs that he directed was the College Chorale. He assumed the directorship from Dr. Edward Meyer in the fall of 1975. The College Chorale comprised 80-120 students who enjoyed singing. "[The Chorale] varied from year to year depending on enrollment, interest and also the director."[167] Every semester was a new story. Since anyone who enjoyed singing could join the College Chorale, the quality of the choir varied from semester to semester with the strength of the singers. This certainly was a challenge for Engel as it would be for any director.

Nonetheless, Meyer recalled that directing the College Chorale was a very successful experience for Engel. Recent students have been required to take one credit of choir as part of the curriculum and participating in this choir fulfilled that requirement. However, at the time when Engel took over the College Chorale, it was an elective choir. Engel directed the College Chorale through the spring of 1977 before passing it on to a new director.[168]

Engel also directed the College Choir during the latter 1970s. He took over the choir in the fall of 1977 from Professor Meilahn Zahn, who preceded Engel as director of the College Choir. Due to health problems, Zahn decided it was time to step down as director of this choir.[169]

The College Choir was the touring choir of DMLC and is still the traveling choir of Martin Luther College (formerly known as Dr. Martin Luther College). This choir gives concert tours every spring to select churches and Lutheran high schools within the WELS. The intent of such tours is to share the gift of quality music with local congregations, share the good news of Jesus and encourage high school students to enroll at DMLC/MLC in preparation for being teachers in the WELS school system and pastors in WELS congregations. This is an elite choir; membership is by audition only.

Engel's choir concerts included a wide variety of choral literature. In Engel's 1980 concert season, his final concert season directing the College Choir, they sang a full and varied program. The concert program was published in the *DMLC Messenger* and was divided into four parts. The pre-concert music was provided by a brass choir which was made up of choir members. The first section included works outlining the life and work of Christ. This section included such works as "Lift Up Your Heads" by Giovanni Gabrieli, "Hodie, Christus Natus Est" by Jan Bender and "This Is the Day" by Jacobus Gallus. The second section focused on the motet "Jesu, Priceless Treasure" by J. S. Bach. The third section consisted of a speech by David Niemi, who was president of the College Choir for that year. He spoke about the mission and purpose of Dr. Martin Luther College. The fourth section, while containing works by earlier composers such as Jan Sweelinck's "Glorify the Lord," tended to focus more on 20th-century choral literature and included "Jubilate" by Egil Hovland and "How Precious" by Daniel Pinkham.

While the choir did the majority of the singing in this program, the congregation and the congregation's children also participated. The Sunday School/Day School children sang "Son of God, Eternal Savior" along with the choir. The congregation participated in the concert by singing along with "Festival Canticle" by Richard Hillert and the hymn concertato "Praise to the Lord" by Paul Manz.[170] This program that was performed by the DMLC College Choir in the spring of 1980 was interesting, varied and educational.

In 1980 Engel decided that he wanted to pursue other projects and take on other responsibilities. His request to step down from the directorship of the College Choir was granted. Professor Roger Hermanson succeeded him as the director of the College Choir in the fall of 1980.[171] (See Appendix A—James Engel at DMLC.)

During the spring break of 1983, Meyer and Engel toured the upper Midwest, giving music and worship lectures geared for the parish musician. (See Appendix D—Letter from James

Engel to Richard Wegner.) "It was the first time, as I recall, that an effort of that type really occurred in [the Wisconsin] Synod."[172] Some of the places where they presented on the tour included North Trinity in Milwaukee (formerly on Villard Street, now closed), St. Mark's in Watertown, St. Paul's in Tomah, and St. John's in Two Rivers. Spring break fell during Lent that year. Engel and Meyer traveled and presented throughout the spring break week. They presented a session every evening for that week. The pace was grueling. Meyer said, "We had a very, very good exchange along the way. [Engel] was a fine person to be with."[173]

Engel presented the lectures and Meyer organized the tour, did the driving and set up each session. "I introduced him but he did the academic work," said Meyer. Each session consisted of two lectures. The first lecture lasted about ninety minutes and usually started around 4:00 p.m. This lecture consisted of expounding upon the role of music in the Church. Engel's presentation was not as complete as he would have preferred but it was a fine introduction to the topic. Meyer felt that Engel was a "fine lecturer."[174]

After the first lecture, the group took time for dinner. Then they settled in for the second ninety-minute lecture that began around 7:00 p.m. This was a practical session where Engel presented selected organ music to attendees. He would play each piece, talk about it and suggest how it might be used in the worship service. "We had scores on hand, just like what Northwestern Publishing House does today. I think that what Northwestern is doing today has its roots in what Jim and I did in 1983 because it hadn't been done before." Meyer started the tour with fifty copies of every score that Engel presented, which resulted in many boxes of music. At the end of each session, Meyer would sell copies to those who wished to purchase them. By the end of the tour, some examples were nearly sold out. "When we got to the last one, we only had a dozen left because they sold out. The amount of organ music that was acquired by organists was just astounding."[175] Meyer handled selling the scores and keeping track of the sales receipts.

Meyer commented that this was the first formal introduction to the massive forty-two-volume *Concordia Hymn Prelude Series*.[176] At the time of their 1983 tour, the first six books of the series were already published. Engel was privileged to have composed twenty-three preludes for this collection. He officially introduced the *Concordia Hymn Prelude Series* to the WELS during this tour. "He was, and saying it in the best sense of the word, pleased to be able to present what he had in the book and the people were really interested too."[177]

Due to the success of these music workshops, Meyer organized a follow-up workshop tour on a grander scale in the summer of 1983. However, Engel did not participate in that tour.[178]

While the Engel family lived in New Ulm, Richard Wegner had the opportunity to play a recital at a church in Edina, Minnesota. The Engels came up from New Ulm to attend the recital and spend the day. While in Minnesota at that time, Wegner took the opportunity to visit the Engels in New Ulm. He recalls the two of them going to a variety of churches and trying out the organs.[179] Dr. Martin Luther College had at least nineteen pipe organs on the campus itself plus the variety of organs in the vicinity of New Ulm. Some of the organs in the churches around New Ulm are historic gems. "Jim and I must have played every organ within the vicinity of New Ulm that day," said Wegner.[180]

One of the curious things that many people have mentioned was that Engel loved to go fishing throughout the time that he taught in New Ulm. While we already know that Engel used to go fishing when he lived in Appleton, he became more widely known for it when he taught at DMLC. He would take some time one day a week so he could have some contemplation time on a lake. Mrs. Engel said, "It gave him time to relax."[181] "He could sit at his office at DMLC and he knew that within an hour, he could be casting his first cast onto the lake where he went fishing."[182] His daughter, Joan, recalls that he used to take a book out with him on the boat. "He didn't care if he caught any fish; it was just the quietness on the lake."[183] Craig Hirschmann remembers talking with Engel about his fishing. Engel said to him, "You know, that's when I do my composing, and I need that rest to do that." Most everyone needs some place to unwind from the stresses, responsibilities and cares of daily life, and fishing on a calm Minnesota lake was Engel's place.[184]

Musical Service at St. John's Lutheran Church, Sleepy Eye, Minnesota

During Engel's tenure at Dr. Martin Luther College, he served as the organist at St. John's Lutheran Church in Sleepy Eye, MN. This is the same Sleepy Eye that is mentioned in the *Little House* books by Laura Ingalls Wilder. Sleepy Eye is located approximately fifteen miles west of New Ulm. Traveling between Sleepy Eye and New Ulm can be difficult during the winter season especially during blizzards. It was not uncommon for U.S. 14 to be officially closed west of New Ulm during a blizzard. Kermit Moldenhauer, music professor at Martin Luther College, New Ulm, MN and former music editor at Northwestern Publishing House, Milwaukee, WI recalls Engel saying: "We've got talent here in New Ulm, let's spread it out a bit."[185] Engel was attracted to playing for this church because it afforded him an opportunity to serve a congregation. There are two WELS churches in the city of New Ulm. They are St. John Lutheran and St. Paul Lutheran. Dr. Martin Luther College had a large organ department. With all of these excellent organists vying to play at the two local churches in New Ulm, there wasn't a huge opportunity for Engel to regularly play for services. St. John in Sleepy Eye gave him that opportunity, and he was an organist there throughout the time that he served at Dr. Martin Luther College. Craig Hirschmann noted that this organ was not a "dream organ." Yet despite the condition of the instrument and the lack of classical resources that he was familiar with at Concordia College in Milwaukee and Gospel Lutheran, Hirschmann commented that Engel enjoyed playing there.[186] Beyond the threat of blizzards, fifteen miles was not really very far to travel during the rest of the year and the back roads made it even more convenient to get there. Not only did Engel play for worship services but he also took care of tuning the organ, similar to what he had done for Gospel Lutheran Church in Milwaukee. Mrs. Engel commented: "When we were at Sleepy Eye, he went to practice every Saturday night. Somebody once asked, 'Does he need to practice?' I joked, 'He practices seven to eight hours a day so he doesn't lose his touch.'"[187] (See Appendix B—St. John Lutheran Church in Sleepy Eye, Minnesota.)

During the time that Engel served as the organist at Sleepy Eye, Mrs. Engel served as a teacher at the church's Lutheran school. She commented about how her husband could easily transpose music to more comfortable keys and how he would sometimes accompany her classes when they sang for church services. Considering the narrow range of children's voices, sight-reading and transposition are great skills to have when accompanying children. They allow for the selection of a wider variety of music that otherwise could not be used. These were the days before organs, digital pianos and electronic keyboards with transposing functions were readily available.[188]

Hirschmann recalls that Engel would have students come out to Sleepy Eye and substitute for him when he could not play for services there. He would not only invite his own students to substitute, but anyone whom he felt was good enough to play in his stead. Engel would also ask students who could play other instruments to help him with worship at Sleepy Eye. Hirschmann recalls that his fellow student, Dr. Lynn (Kitzerow) Petersen, would sometimes play the organ and other times play the violin at St. John's. "He made quite a practice of using the student talent at Sleepy Eye."[189]

Hirschmann recalls some advice that Engel gave him regarding the purchasing of music books. "He said, 'When I purchase an organ book and I'm using my organ money to buy that book, I always put down where I got that organ money in the front of the book.'" Engel asked him to play for a funeral at Sleepy Eye. When Hirschmann received the check, he purchased some *Parish Organist* books and did exactly as Engel had advised. "I put down 'Purchased from … Money from St. John's Sleepy Eye' in the front of the book."[190]

Hirschmann also recalls a charming story about subbing for Engel, without transportation and in the middle of a blizzard.

> One time he wanted me to play for morning services in Sleepy Eye and I didn't have a car. I would normally get a ride from one of my friends or work something else out, but there was no way I was getting a ride that Sunday. I told him that I didn't have a car. My friends who would normally lend me a car were not able to lend it to me that Sunday. It just wasn't working out. He said, "Take mine." The funny part about this story was that the one time I had his car, it was a snowy morning and we are talking drifts. It was blowing and impossible. I turned around,

called the pastor and said there is no way I can make it. I don't even recall what happened, if they had services, but he certainly understood and told me "don't even try it." It was one of those things. I remember that he was willing to lend his car to a student. He was a very generous kind of man.[191]

Engel's Role in the Development of a New Hymnal for the Wisconsin Synod

Engel also played a role in the eventual production of a new hymnal for the WELS. His expertise was first utilized during the *Sampler* project. The *Sampler* project was part of the New/Revised Hymnal Project. The *Sampler: New Hymns and Liturgy* was published in 1986 as a way for the Wisconsin Synod to test a revised liturgy and new hymns. It was also a wonderful tool to get WELS parishioners prepared for the changes that would come with a new hymnal. It contained a liturgy for the Common Service based on pages five and fifteen in *The Lutheran Hymnal*, twelve psalms with psalm tones from *Lutheran Worship*, and twenty-one hymns that were not contained in *The Lutheran Hymnal*. Rev. Kurt Eggert, director of the hymnal project, asked Engel to help him prepare musical settings for the *Sampler*. However, "[he] had no official capacity with the project."[192] Rev. Victor Prange, chair of the *Sampler* liturgy committee of the Commission on Worship, shared the following regarding Engel's role in the project from his diary.

> The first mention I have of Engel in my diary is on May 30-31, 1986. On the evening of May 30th, I report that "the Liturgy Committee met to make changes in The Service which were suggested by Eggert and Jim Engel who harmonized the liturgy. We worked till 11:00 p.m." The next morning the Joint Hymnal Committee went to a church "to hear it played based on the accompaniment of Engel."[193]

Prange further comments that Engel was not present when the *Sampler* liturgy was presented to the Liturgy Committee. The Commission on Worship approved the Sampler liturgy June 2, 1986.[194] Engel is credited with setting the harmonization for the hymn, "Son of God, Eternal Savior" (LORD, REVIVE US) in the *Sampler*.

One curious item found in the *Sampler*, and attributed to Engel, is a minor change made to the melody line of the *Gloria in excelsis*. (Heavn'ly King) *(See Example 1)*. Moldenhauer comments on this melodic alteration. "I suppose [Engel] will be forever remembered as changing to B-natural to B-flat in the *Gloria*. It still comes up in class: Why do we do that? ... and I don't have a good answer."[195] The B-natural that outlined the harmonic pattern of I-V7/V- V was replaced by the B-flat. Some WELS musicians have liked this change, while others have not. This change is also found in the Common Service found in *Christian Worship*.

Example 1

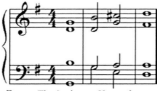 

From: *The Lutheran Hymnal*   From: *Sampler & Christian Worship*

"Eggert suffered a heart attack in the fall of 1986. It became increasingly obvious that he needed help."[196] In September, 1987, at the request of Eggert, the Commission on Worship suggested that the Conference of Presidents appoint Engel as the music editor of the hymnal project.[197] The Conference of Presidents is the primary body responsible for the doctrine and practice of the WELS and consists of the synod president and the presidents of each district. "The Conference of Presidents responded positively to the commission's request and appointed Engel to the position of part-time music consultant."[198] Engel's duties were to "review music manuscripts of liturgies and hymns and be responsible for the final form of music manuscripts prior to publication, and to advise and assist the project director and committees regarding the production of liturgical music and hymns."[199] During his time as consultant, Engel dedicated much energy to the hymnal project. Mrs. Engel recalls that Engel would travel to Milwaukee once a month and also to Minneapolis once a month. "It took a lot of time and had him out on the road often."[200] She also recalls him copying a lot of music that he was intending to review and that he was very dedicated to the hymnal project. Moldenhauer recalls: "I remember him being around, and then also communicating with us on things he thought should be done with music, with hymnody and so forth."[201] Members of the hymnal project would often go to church music conferences and lectures. It was on one of these lectures the following story takes place.

> Early in the project, Moldenhauer and Engel went to a conference at Concordia College—River Forest, IL. We were at the opening lecture, and it must have been early in the hymnal project, because we sat in on Morning Prayer at Concordia River-Forest and I remember Jim and I [sic] coming out... and we just loved what had happened in that service. We were talking and he said, "I sure hope we can do something like this." So he had this kind of goal in mind of trying to achieve something that was worthwhile.[202]

Regarding the subject of notating music by computer, Moldenhauer recalls that Engel was in the forefront of exploring the possibilities of the computer program, Finale. "I do know that in between the sampler and the hymnal he was the person who was really looking into how emerging technologies could be used in order to produce the hymnal."[203] Engel relayed to Moldenhauer about a trip which he took to Schmitt Music in the Twin Cities. Engel was able to test an Apple computer which had one of the first versions of Finale installed on it. This was a time when Apple computers had small screens, so it was not as easy to work with as our present-day computers with increasingly large screens. The hymnal committee was considering whether it was worthwhile to buy one of these systems and Engel strongly encouraged its usage. This occurred sometime in late 1987 or in 1988, during his time as music consultant. "I remember hearing of that system and wondering how we were going to get it to work. It was such a primitive system."[204] Northwestern Publishing House eventually purchased the technology to engrave music and entered into the music publishing industry. Northwestern currently publishes church music by a variety of well-known composers, as well as works by new composers. Moldenhauer believes that

Engel's research on this new engraving technology directly influenced Northwestern's decision to produce *Christian Worship: A Lutheran Hymnal* in-house.[205]

It was Engel's goal to provide the best worship resources and music for the Lutheran Church in general and the Wisconsin Synod in particular. It was Engel's belief, along with the hymnal committee, that providing quality worship materials would greatly help to achieve that goal.[206] Through the work of Engel, and all the dedicated members of the hymnal committee, many congregations in the WELS have made progress towards the use of quality worship music, but there is always more progress to be made.

Engel's Illness and Death

It is unfortunate that Engel became ill with what was soon diagnosed as lung cancer (he was a life-long smoker) in the late fall of 1988, only a little over a year after becoming music consultant on the hymnal project. As he became more ill, he was not able to be as active in the project as he would have liked. Moldenhauer recalls, "It was really a hard time for us because we felt so badly for him."[207] Unfortunately, he was too ill to help with the major music editing that was coming to the forefront during that time.

The sudden illness and subsequent death of Engel came as a sad shock to his family, friends and students. Hirschmann recalls talking with Engel on the phone just before Engel found out about his illness. Engel told Hirschmann that he could not get rid of a cold that he had developed.[208] Wegner recalls making a phone call to Engel when he was being treated in a hospital in Minneapolis.[209] Geis vividly recalls the circumstances surrounding her father's illness:

> All was well until December of 1988. At that time our family had gotten together for a Christmas celebration in New Ulm. Dad didn't look well. He was suffering from a respiratory infection and a cough. He was very tired. We stayed through the holidays and reluctantly left New Ulm, knowing that Dad was going to see his doctor. Soon after, we heard of his diagnosis of cancer and were very surprised and quite devastated. I was getting ready to get married in July of 1989 and Dad was picking out organ music for

my wedding. However, God had other plans for him. Dad passed away in the spring, well before my wedding day.[210]

Engel died on Monday, April 17, 1989, from lung cancer. "He died with the Lord's Prayer on his lips, hands folded, my mother at his bedside, his children close by."[211] His funeral service was held on April 20, 1989, at St. Paul's Lutheran Church in New Ulm, MN. According to the service folder, great hymns and anthems of hope and joy were sung that day. (See Appendix D—Engel's Funeral Bulletin.) "At Dad's funeral, the college choirs sang. They filled the church with the sounds of those familiar, treasured hymns of his childhood."[212] Engel's "I Walk with Angels" was sung, along with Hans Leo Hassler's "Lord, Let at Last Thine Angels Come." Hymns included "Christ Jesus Lay in Death's Strong Bands" and "This Joyful Eastertide." It is fitting that "This Joyful Eastertide" was sung since it was from the *Sampler*.

The author was pleased to talk with Mr. Dale Witte who had attended Engel's funeral. He is currently the music director at Winnebago Lutheran Academy and is active as a composer and served on the psalms committee for the new WELS hymnal 2021. At the time of Engel's passing, Witte was a student at Dr. Martin Luther College. He sang for Engel's funeral as part of the DMLC College Choir.

We sang Hans Leo Hassler's double choir motet on *Lord, Let at Last Thine Angels Come.* Many of us in the choir had had Engel for Theory and Counterpoint, so it was especially hard for us, his former students, to sing for his funeral. To make matters worse, the College Choir was seated in the church (St. Paul's, New Ulm) down front on the right in the choir pews which faced perpendicular to the main axis of the church, in full view of the casket, the family and the pastor at all times. Prof. Roger Hermanson was our choir director and knew that many of us were getting choked up during the rehearsals in the days leading up to the funeral. He told us that it was our job for that funeral not to get choked up—it would be the hardest thing for us to do, but also the most important so that we could proclaim the hope of heaven that the motet so beautifully and confidently put to music. That song still is one of my all-time-favorite pieces of choir music because of the memories surrounding that performance.[213]

Engel was buried at St. Paul's Lutheran Cemetery in Mt. Prospect, Illinois where Mrs. Engel grew up and where they were married. She had the following text engraved on his gravestone. "With Christ, my Savior, Guide, and angel hosts beside for all the world I would not stay; My walk is Heav'nward all the way." This text comes from Engel's composition: "I Walk with Angels," which he dedicated to his wife, Norma.[214] These words are a fitting summary to Engel's life, for he did indeed walk with angels throughout his life and continues to walk with them still.

Remembrances of Engel

Family Life in the Engel Home

One can read all the facts of a person's life and still not get a full idea of the personality and character of that person. While the author never knew Engel, he had the opportunity to communicate with many people who knew him: members of his family, friends, colleagues and students. Through anecdotes and summaries of conversations, the author wishes to convey a sense of who Engel was as a person.

The author communicated with four members of Engel's family. These members are: Janet Engel, Engel's sister; Norma Engel, his wife; and two of his daughters, Joan Mueller and Mary Geis. Beyond facts, they were able to share who Engel was as a person. Engel was primarily a kind, gentle servant of the living God. His whole life, no matter what he was doing, was spent in loving service to his Savior, Jesus. He shared this love with his family and everyone he worked with. His family has said this, his colleagues have said it and his students have said it. His daughter, Mary Geis, put it this way:

> First and foremost, my father was a man who loved the Lord. He knew his Savior. He understood and accepted the concept of faith through grace. This knowledge was CENTRAL in his life and he wanted to make sure his family had this knowledge as well. He married a Christian woman. My brother and sisters and I were baptized. We went to church. We prayed together. We talked about God.[215]

Engel loved his family and, despite being very busy with his work, made sure to spend time with them and be a loving father and husband. Geis told the author that the family used to go ice-skating in the park across the street during the winter months. Ice-skating was something that he had enjoyed doing as a child and now enjoyed doing with his family. She also said they used to go on summer picnics as a family in the park. There were also times when the family would go to a beach on the shore of Lake Michigan and grill burgers and hot dogs. They also swam in the water. Geis commented that the lake water was "icy cold." The family would also periodically go to the drive-in theater to watch a movie. On Sunday afternoons when it was raining outside, the Engel family played Monopoly.

> Our one-week summer vacation "up north" was one of my Dad's favorite events. We packed up the car (suitcases strapped to the hood of our old station wagon) and drove up to Little Corn Lake. We rented a cabin with a big kitchen and two bedrooms (one for Dad and Mom and one for the kids). We fished all day and played cards well into the night. Is there anything better than fresh caught fish for supper seven days in a row? My father was in seventh heaven—and the rest of us were glad to have him all to ourselves![216]

The Engel children attended Lutheran day schools and Lutheran high schools. As Mary pointed out, this was an act of love because the cost of going to Lutheran schools was significant for four children on a teacher's salary, which was not very large. The Engels not only sent their children to Lutheran schools but also took an active role in their education. They were interested in what their children were learning and how well they did in school. They also helped their children with school projects. Some of these projects could be quite complex. Geis recalls a couple specific examples where her father took a direct interest in her studies:

> During the school year, my Dad often talked with me about my lessons. Once he did not like what I was being taught in my high school religion class and he insisted on coming to school with me for a meeting with the teacher! On another occasion, he almost built a second harpsichord for a science fair project of mine in which

we successfully attempted to demonstrate the sympathetic vibration of harpsichord strings. For this, WE received a blue ribbon![217]

Engel's love of music and humility in the face of personal glory was also very apparent. To him music had a divine purpose over and above enjoyment or entertainment. Music was intended to give glory to God and should always be done to the best of a person's ability. Geis commented on this:

> Dad and his choirs participated in many concerts and programs in Milwaukee. Our family attended these events together as often as possible. I specifically remember his college choir singing the words of Handel's *Messiah* in the Concordia College gymnasium. I was in high school at the time. It was so moving that we all had tears streaming down our faces. I was so proud that I thought I would burst. My Dad, in his usual humble manner, was very pleased with the outcome of this concert but did not stay around long for the hand shaking and praise afterwards. He never wanted the attention for himself. His focus was worship. He did it to honor his Creator.[218]

Since Engel was a consummate musician, one might expect that the Engel children were musically trained, which was true. All of Engel's children were involved in music. Some sang in choirs and all of them studied the piano sometime in their lives. "All of us took piano lessons from Dad at one time or another."[219] Geis shared some wonderful stories about studying music with her father. The first concerns piano lessons.

> First, I was quite shy and sensitive as a young girl. I had a tendency to cry if Dad had to correct my piano playing. This was not okay with him! Therefore, for two years I took piano lessons from a teacher in the public school system so that he did not have to see me cry! Fortunately, eventually I got over my sensitivities![220]

The second story concerns practice time. As every musician will attest, practice is a vital part of learning to play a musical instrument well. The act of practicing can be a tedious affair. However, in the Engel household, practice often became more enjoyable when Engel joined in the practice session.

> Sometimes Dad would break up a boring, tedious practice session by joining in the practice. I would play my simple tune and he would play something jazzy and fun as an accompaniment, turning a half hour practice into a wonderful duet! I am happy to say that Dad and I played duets for the entire time I lived at home. All I had to do was sit down at the keyboard and play a note or two. This was his cue! If at all possible, he would join me on the piano bench and we would have some musical fun.[221]

Geis also relayed how her dad used to allow her special honor on Sunday mornings during the time the Engel family lived in Milwaukee. This tradition lasted for a number of years while Geis was growing up. This was obviously something very dear to her.

> On Sundays Dad would wake me up early and we would drive to church to attend services together. There were three services each Sunday at Gospel Lutheran Church. As a very special treat, he would let me play the last note of the very last song of each service. Surely everybody was out of the church by then, so if I made a mistake it would not be noticed. I would slide onto the seat next to him and somehow he would point to the note I was to play. This was a tricky thing for him to do because he was playing with both hands and feet at the same time! I don't remember when this tradition began or ended. I just remember it was a very good time of my life and it lasted for quite a few years.[222]

During the time the Engel family lived in Appleton, James Jr. and Joan were of high school age and attended Fox Valley Lutheran. Engel made sure to spend quality time with both of them. Engel was heavily involved in Joan's high school singing career and mentored her. He also spent time with James, Jr. in a boat on a nearby lake. They were fishing partners and this provided them with the time to do some father/son bonding. As Geis commented: "What a nice balance!"[223] One can see through these recolle ctions that Professor and Mrs. Engel provided a loving, God-fearing household. The Lord was first and foremost in their lives.

Engel as a Respected Christian Teacher

Engel was also a friend and Christian example for his students. Jeanine Heller, an alumna of Dr. Martin Luther College, writes that Engel "had a deep faith in God." "I noticed that he bowed his head in prayer before playing the organ in a public setting. He would talk about playing music for the glory of God."[224] Engel would go out of his way to visit his students when they were sick. Jeanine recalls that Engel came to visit her in the hospital when she had pneumonia.[225] As mentioned earlier, Engel let Hirschmann borrow his car so he could travel to Sleepy Eye, MN to play the organ for a worship service. While at Concordia College in Milwaukee, he invited students over to his house. These are all examples of the kind, friendly and Christian man that Engel was.

Engel is remembered by his students as a wonderful man and an excellent teacher. He had a wide range of knowledge and interests. He was a teacher, a church musician, a fisherman, had a love for sports, knew how to construct and repair things around his house and had wide variety of other interests. "He was well-rounded and I think he tried to encourage that too, that you became a well-rounded individual and did not become too specialized. That was also his appeal. I think he could have carried on a conversation with anybody."[226] Jeanine Heller recalls that Engel was energetic, always "on the go" and walked at a very brisk pace. However, his voice was calm, patient and reassuring. He went out of his way to help people."[227]

> While Jim has been with our Lord for almost twenty years, I still remember him vividly. He always struck me as a very devout gentleman, always ready to sit down and talk. He was a very humble man, even to the extent of composing/arranging music for the all-male choir, and rarely submitting it for publication.[228]

Engel was definitely respected and appreciated by his students.

Engel as a Respected Colleague

Faculty members who taught with Engel respected him for his ability and kind, Christian demeanor. "He was a kind, loving, caring man who never spoke disparagingly of another."[229] Balko also recalled that Engel was an "outstanding musician, teacher and person." While Balko does not recall that Engel did a lot of composing during his Concordia years, "what he did was of a high standard."[230] Moldenhauer commented that the both faculty and students highly respected Engel. "There was a real respect for his work—in theory, composition, organ and choral directing. Everybody that I know that had him speaks very highly of him."[231]

Engel was a highly respected and well-loved individual. He was an excellent teacher, musician, and composer. Yet, because he did not call attention to himself, average people would not necessarily realize the knowledge and expertise Engel possessed had they met him on the street. He was a humble, family man who, while using his talents and abilities, would not flaunt them. He was not an outspoken man, but when he did speak, people would listen and appreciate his point of view. When he did express his point of view, it was expressed with a thoughtfulness which was respected by his peers. He loved his family and cared about his students. Most of all, he dedicated his life in loving service to his Lord and Savior, Jesus Christ. This was James Edward Engel.

Engel's Work

. . . as a Music Teacher

Engel was known for being an excellent and caring teacher by his students and colleagues. Meyer commented that Engel was "a very much respected teacher." When he was on campus, he was always busy. He was so busy, in fact, that he would run between buildings without wearing a coat in winter. "It wasn't until his last year of life, when he stopped teaching in January of 1989 that I ever saw him put on an overcoat."[232] As mentioned earlier, Engel had an equal share of student advisees, a fair class load, and normal faculty committee work—all of those activities which were expected of faculty members. As a faculty member, Meyer commented that Engel rarely spoke up at general faculty meetings but had plenty to say at music division meetings. "When he spoke, people listened and respected his opinions."[233] "Jim was a very introspective man. If one wanted to know the thoughts of Engel, one had to ask questions. He seldom engaged in conversation with impulsive thought. Having this trait, however, one would always listen attentively when he spoke."[234] Meyer, when he was the chairman of the music department at DMLC, knew that Engel was doing a proper job of teaching his students and that all of the other faculty work was being done to the best of Engel's ability. He went about his work of teaching without any real pomp and circumstance but everything that he did was done well.

Engel lived his love of music and readily shared it with his students. Balko commented: "As a teacher, there are few that could match the standard of Engel. I was very much aware of student's positive testimonies while at Concordia College. He possessed a combination of high expectation and patience that I always envied."[235]

The comments and stories which were told by Engel's students are found in the following sections.

. . . as a **Choral Director**

As was mentioned earlier, Brenda Glodowski was a student of Engel's when he taught at Fox Valley Lutheran High School. He inspired her to study music in college and become a choral director. Glodowski currently teaches music at West Lutheran High School in the Minneapolis/St. Paul, Minnesota area. She specifically recalled Engel's passion for music as a major inspiration for her study of music.

> He would expound on the music. You could always tell when he was going to take a moment where he felt he needed to talk to us about what was going on in the music, talk about what he wanted us to express through the music or what he felt the message was that we needed to convey. You could always tell because he would pause, sit down on his stool, take off his glasses and run his hands through his hair. It was just that little bit of nonverbal communication. OK, he's going to talk to us about the music now. I remember always getting very excited about those moments anticipating what insight was he going to share? What passion was he going to share? I've always loved singing in music my whole life, but he was the one who got me excited about choral music and what a director can do—working with young people to help them express their faith through music.[236]

Mrs. Engel and her daughter, Joan Mueller, also mentioned that Engel did this in his choral practice sessions. He would often take time to explain to his choirs what the purpose of the music was and how the choir could work to interpret the music to make it meaningful to everyone. Mrs. Engel and Mueller relayed a story that exemplifies this. There was a time when the choir just was not responding to the music in the way that Engel felt they should. At times like that, Mueller recalls that he would often stop and say, "Let's stop here for a moment and think about what we're singing."[237] In this case, he sat down and took the time to explain the meaning of the piece and why it should be sung a certain way. It was one of those kinds of pieces with a lot of meaning and Engel's explanation of it was very touching to us. Mrs. Engel recalls her husband saying that: "There were tears in everybody's eyes."[238]

Throughout his career, Engel directed his choirs with enthusiasm and intensity. Mahnke explained how the typical choral rehearsal went when he attended Concordia College, Milwaukee:

> We had rehearsals daily, immediately following morning chapel. Engel would begin the rehearsal fully and *neatly* dressed: dress shirt, necktie tied, sport coat on. As the rehearsals progressed, the sport coat was the first to go; then, the sleeves of the shirt got rolled up; the necktie was loosened. By the end of the rehearsal, the shirt was often partially untucked and Engel looked like he had been through a battle. He put his entire self into the music during the rehearsals; his effort showed in the results.[239]

This basic rehearsal style, as described by Mahnke, did not change much when Engel taught at Dr. Martin Luther College. Jeanine Heller shares some comments with us about that time. "Engel directed his choirs with great enthusiasm and energy. He would bounce up and down on his toes when directing a light or lively piece. I still use some of his vocal warm-up exercises with my own choir."[240]

Through the years, Engel directed a variety of choral groups: grade school choirs, church choirs, high school choirs and college choirs. Through these choirs, he shared his love of music with his students and church members. His choir members appreciated his abilities and learned much about music through him. He inspired the best in his choir members.

. . . as an Organ Professor

Engel taught organ lessons throughout his professional career. He started teaching students how to play the organ after graduating from Concordia, River Forest and continued teaching the instrument his whole life. He primarily taught organ students associated with schools where he taught but also taught private lessons.

Jeffrey Hammes took organ lessons with Engel for "two or three years." While he was not a Concordia student, Hammes took private lessons from Engel on Concordia's chapel organ Saturday mornings.[241]

Hammes commented that Engel was always "very encouraging and gracious." There were also times during lessons when they would converse more about the music than actually play the music.[242] It was important to Engel for his students to understand the nature and style of the music and not just how to play it. Hammes further commented about his organ lessons with Engel.

> Since I was an independent student, he pretty much let me guide the directions we went in with regard to music. I was interested in 20th-century organ music at the time, so I learned some stuff by Jan Bender with him. And it was during this time that I developed a real interest and liking for the music of Paul Hindemith. I learned the first movement of the Hindemith second organ sonata during that time.[243]

Glenn Mahnke, when he was a student at Concordia College in Milwaukee, also took organ lessons from Engel. Mahnke had taken lessons from one of the other organ instructors on campus, but since he was in the pastoral track, he did not feel he needed to take organ lessons during his sophomore year. Before the completion of the first semester of that year, Mahnke switched majors and decided that he wanted to study church music and education. Engel, who was his academic advisor, told him that organ lessons were essential to his new course of study. "He insisted that I immediately begin taking organ lessons from him. During the semester I worked with him, Jim managed to move me through about two full years of lessons, getting me ready to continue at Concordia, River Forest as a junior in college."[244]

Jeanine Heller took organ lessons from Engel when she was a student at Dr. Martin Luther College. Engel was her instructor throughout her time at DMLC, from 1975 until 1980. "I consider him to be one of the greatest teachers I've known. Engel had the ability to motivate me to practice organ and strive to be the best musician that I could be, because that is what he did."[245]

A common theme which family members and former students relayed was that Engel used to spend a lot of time practicing for services and occasional recitals. "He practiced what he preached. I remember him saying that when he was a grade school teacher, he would get up early to practice one or two hours in the morning before school."[246] Heller commented that Engel admired the work of the Baroque composers. J. S. Bach was one of his favorites. "[Engel] told me that on the first Sunday of Advent he would always play Bach's 'Savior of the Nations, Come.' He said that if a musician is going to put in time practicing, he should practice great music such as the works of Bach."[247]

Heller became an undergraduate organ instructor at DMLC between her Junior and Senior years. Engel spoke on her behalf so that she could have this rare opportunity. [The author noted that Engel, himself, was asked to stay on an extra year at Concordia, River Forest, to teach organ and piano.] Engel also helped her prepare for her own solo college recital.[248]

Kenneth Lehman was an organ student of Engel's in the early 1980s and a contemporary of Craig Hirschmann. He took three years of lessons with Engel although he had no previous organ experience before attending DMLC. Lehman always wanted to take organ lessons but did not have that opportunity until he went to college. He had taken enough piano lessons so that the transition to organ was easily within his reach. To Engel, there was more to life on campus than just music lessons. Lehman was also a member of the DMLC basketball team. Engel would often attend the home games and, when Lehman would come in for lessons, Engel would often ask him how the team was doing. They would spend only about a minute or so talking, but this personal touch was enough to help Lehman relax and ease into the organ lesson. When a student would make a mistake, Engel would not try to make the student feel bad about it. He would rather suggest better ways of playing things. Engel focused on presenting positive solutions to the problems his students were having. His goal was to help his students accomplish the challenges that they faced. Engel would demonstrate technique (such as pedaling) when it was necessary and have his student try it. Lehman also recalls that Engel taught him how to modulate from one key to another—including the use of diminished chords as a pivot point to progress into the new key. The trick was to make the change into the new key as seamless and inconspicuous as possible. Lehman noted how easy it was for Engel to accomplish this. It was very hard to detect the pivot chord where one key transitioned into another because Engel was so smooth at performing modulations.[249]

Mr. Craig Hirschmann was a student at Dr. Martin Luther College in the early 1980s and took organ lessons from Engel throughout his years of study at DMLC. He was very pleased to have Engel as his organ instructor. Hirschmann recalled many details about his lessons with Engel that were enlightening. He said that Engel did not play much during his lessons. Since Engel's goal was to let his students "discover" the music, he would not completely play a piece for his student. "Occasionally he would play just a phrase or something, but basically it was by word of mouth, trying to draw it out of you."[250] This method of discussing the music with his students and letting them discover the inner meaning of the music was a common theme among the students with whom the author talked.

Engel tended towards a smooth style of playing which he taught to his students. The key to musicality was that the music was cleanly played and there was never any doubt that Engel's playing was musical. Hirschmann recalls learning to playing Bach's transcription of Vivaldi's Concerto No. 4. "...and when I switched manuals, it was pretty legato. I mean, the way he had it fingered. He taught me pretty much to play on the Swell and then there would almost be this connection to go down to the Great."[251] Hirschmann recalls that when he played this piece for an organ jury, one of the professors at the jury commented that his method of playing this piece was an out-of-date practice and wondered who had taught him to play it that way. The style Engel had taught Hirschmann was musically appropriate and he had played the piece cleanly.

However, Engel did admit at a subsequent lesson that there were other ways this piece could be played. There could be more of a break when switching manuals. "We could open it up a little more and it would still be musical. Just watch out though that you don't interrupt the tactus [or tempo]."[252] The most important thing that Engel wished to impress upon Hirschmann was that music, no matter how it was played, should be performed musically.

At the same time, Engel was an avid reader and read the latest scholarship from books and journals. He was conversant in the latest theories about the performance of music throughout music history. Hirschmann recalls that Engel told him to put "definite 'détaché'" (or slightly detached notes) into the Bach pieces that he was playing. Engel used the term "brittle" to describe quality of sound that he wanted for the Bach pieces. "I remember him saying 'loosen up the arm—more brittle.' He wanted more 'détaché' in my technique."[253] This detached method of playing Baroque music was based on scholarship published during the 1960s and 1970s. Engel was not only aware of the latest research but was teaching these newer interpretations to his students.

Hirschmann recalled his first lesson with Engel at DMLC. He had been playing for four years and was already a good organist. "I was quite adept at playing services," said Hirschmann. There were two Schlicker practice organs located on the lower level of the Music Center and his lesson was held on one of those. Engel asked him to play a piece, which he did. Engel, with a suit and tie on, "got on his hands and knees and crawled from this side to that side." Hirschmann recalls thinking to himself, "What are you doing?" When he was finished playing, Engel got back up and said; "you are playing too far back from the black keys. Your foot swings back and forth. You've got to play this far from the black keys and only that much onto the black keys so you minimize that movement." He knew at that moment that he would need to modify and improve his pedal technique. Hirschmann recalls: "Well, that threw my spacing and confidence off. It was a struggle to adapt to that but I was determined to do it. He emphasized toe/heel pedaling."[254]

While at Dr. Martin Luther College, Hirschmann played J. S. Bach's *Prelude and Fugue in D-Major* as part of a master class with Dr. David Craighead. He recalls using a toe/heel technique for the pedal passages— "toe, heel (left foot) and then right toe, left heel cross—and then I worked up the scale for that opening passage. When Craighead saw it, he said: 'alternate toes going up to even it out.' Engel was kind of smiling." So Hirschmann tried the alternating toe technique that Craighead had suggested and felt that did even out the passage. "[Craighead] brought up that many organists play all toes for this piece but he did not have a problem with how it was performed toe/heel because it sounded clean." In the same piece, Engel had Hirschmann "do little echo effects in the *Alla Breve* section in the middle of the prelude." He played the piece, including the echo effects, and Craighead thought it was a good effect. "He said, 'They are interesting and they engage the listener.' But he said that in an organ where there is a definite separation of divisions, he felt it would be too distracting. If all of the divisions are kind of homogenous, from a single source, you can get away with that. However, one should not do that if you're going to have an organ where the divisions are spatially separated. It would be like overdoing it."[255] The "Echo" effect could easily become distracting to the listener and take away from the overall musical effect.

Engel did not impose his own fingering on his student by writing it into the score right away. He felt that his students should explore and use the fingering that works best for that individual. He took a practical approach to fingering in that everyone is different and one fingering style does not always transfer from one student to another. "You should be able to play a piece without putting your fingers in knots. If there is an easier way to play it with the same effect, then go with it."[256] Once his students had determined their best fingering, then they would write them in the score.

Hirschmann commented that Engel taught his students how to decorate their hymns and modulate from the original key to a new key between the stanzas of hymns. Decorations would include passing tones and even alternate harmonizations. Hirschmann recalled this example from his lessons. "I remember going through 'Praise to the Lord, the Almighty' and he made me come up with a modulation." The last stanza was to be played a whole step higher than what was written in the hymnal. "And I had to learn by just looking at the hymnal and not writing it out. He made me use it for chapel so that I could gain some confidence. That worked well for me."[257] Hirschmann saved a modulation chart that Engel had written up for him as a part of one of his lessons. (See Appendix D—Modulation Chart written for Mr. Craig Hirschmann by James Engel.)

Engel helped Hirschmann prepare for his junior recital. Since DMLC seniors traditionally went out into the field to accomplish their student teaching requirement for a full semester, a student who intended to perform a capstone recital would be required to present this in his/her junior year. Hirschmann said that the whole timetable during a student's senior year was far too disruptive to also focus on a senior recital. The program for the recital was to be a broad cross-section of organ literature. It included works by Nicolas Bruhns, J. S. Bach, F. J. Haydn, César Franck and others. Specific works included selections from Haydn's *Musical Clocks*, chosen for their fun and light nature, and the great *Chorale in B-Minor* by Franck. Hirschmann described the challenges of putting this program together, along with the challenges of learning Franck's *Chorale in B-Minor:*

> Originally we were going to do Hindemith's *Sonata II* and I also think some Pepping. My dad listened to the program and said that this was really boring. I had a great respect for my dad, and yet I was afraid of offending Engel. I don't know what broke the ice, but I just laid it on him that my dad thought that this was just a tedious program. He kind of had a smile on his face and said: "Well, sometime these recitals up here can get quite academic." I remember that that was the adjective he used. He said "maybe we can do something about that." We came up with this program and I really think it was a crowd pleaser because you can't go wrong with Bach or any of these guys. This piece [*The Musical Clocks*] lightened the program up with its novel registrations. The *Chorale in B-Minor*, my dad didn't like at first, but the more he listened to it, it became a favorite of his—and me too. DMLC, at the time I attended, really emphasized German Baroque literature. You almost never knew what the swell pedal was for. Was it the clutch? You had no idea what the thing was. I guess a person knew what it did but it was almost anathema to use it. It was almost as if using it would be a slide into romanticism and somehow your playing was ruined. When I first was learning the Franck—"open the swell pedal, close the swell pedal." Well, I was not used to all of this and he really laid into me. "You really have got to get better at that or we can not play this piece," and I was completely overwhelmed at the start. But time passed and it got better. Using the swell pedal was really good for me. At

least I felt it was a quantum leap forward, at least for my playing. I hadn't really used it before, except maybe to balance divisions between each other if I had to, if I was at a church where that was needed for services.[258]

Engel not only taught his students to be organists, he composed music for them to play. According to Hirschmann, Lehman and Heller, he would write hymn intonations for his students to play for chapel services at Dr. Martin Luther College. Some of these works were eventually published while others were not. Some students would talk with Engel and say, "I can't find anything to play on this hymn." The next thing that student would know was that there would be a piece ready for that student to play—at his or her playing level. Lehman recalls playing for chapel. He mentioned to Engel what the hymn for the day would be and a couple hours later Engel would have an intonation written for him to play for the service. "He said that if I wanted to make changes on it, go ahead, but there were never any changes I would want to make. It was just beautiful."[259] Lehman commented that Engel always made the melody audible so that the hymn could be properly introduced. He sometimes used pedal-point, two-part, trio style, whatever he felt would best fit the hymn and could be written in a short period of time. Heller shares one of her experiences with us regarding a composition that Engel wrote for her:

> Engel composed an original piece specifically for my organ recital. It was based on the Christmas hymn melody "All Praise to Thee, Eternal God" (GELOBET SEIST DU, JESU CHRIST) and was a challenging piece of music. He liked the sound of repeated fourths. The piece that Engel wrote for my recital was composed in 1979, the year I gave my recital in May. He told me that he submitted it for publication but it was not accepted at that time.[260]

For those students whom Engel saw had compositional talent, he would encourage them to write their own pieces to use in chapel services. "For some students he would say, 'You should write something on that' and then he wouldn't write you anything."[261] Composition was a skill that Engel fostered in his students. It is a skill that serves the busy church musician well. Engel encouraged his students to follow the examples of Theodore Beck. Theodore Beck's *76 Preludes* was a good model because he composed in a variety of compositional styles that were easy for students to emulate. "It was kind of like a little primer of examples. Engel suggested that we buy a copy and even use it as a model for our own compositions."[262] A number of Engel's former students became composers.

Engel always encouraged his students and tried to instill in them the attitude that no matter what level of musicianship each student had, the student should always do his/her best and give God the glory. "There were better organists than me at DMLC but he always made me feel like I could [be an excellent organist]."[263] However, he could be unhappy with students who were not living up to their potential. Such students were a frustration to Engel because those students did not give their best. It did not matter what level of proficiency his students had. As long as his students put their best effort into their studies, Engel would be pleased.

Finally, Engel was an example to his organ students. While he was not known for performing organ recitals on the DMLC campus, he played for many chapel services and played at St. John Evangelical Lutheran Church in Sleepy Eye. Hirschmann comments: "He was always flawless every time he played for chapel. Honestly, my jaw dropped every time. I always had the desire to hear him play a full-length recital, but I never saw that happen."[264] It is unknown to the author why Engel did not play full-length recitals in New Ulm. If a person wanted to hear Engel perform a recital when he served at DMLC, that person had to go to recitals that he performed off campus—primarily organ dedication recitals. In his earlier years at Concordia, he was well-known for his service playing, even more-so than a recitalist. He was an accomplished organist and had excellent playing technique. "Jim never seemed to have a problem playing the instrument. While he was rather short, and had short, stubby fingers, he played with ease and great skill. His pedal technique was interesting from the standpoint that he could play fast pedal parts well in wingtips!"[265] Engel was known for his ability to inspire congregations to new heights of praise. "Jim's organ playing in a worship service could arouse a congregation to sing like few other church musicians. Jim had a gift of communicating to the average worshiper without being trite. He was a master at chorale improvisation. His love for serving his Lord and those who joined him in song never ended. This was his life.[266] The excellence that he showed during worship services is the same excellence that he attempted to instill in his students. Engel proved to be a model for his students to follow. He led them by his example.

During the mid-1980s, Engel created *A Manual for the Beginning Organist* as a training manual for his organ students. As part of the process, he consulted with his fellow professors at DMLC. On the title page of this manual is found this description, "the careful review of the initial copies of this manual by my colleagues, Dr. Edward Meyer, Professors Charles Luedtke, Fred Bartel, and Joyce Schubkegel is herewith acknowledged. Their valuable suggestions and encouragement were greatly appreciated."[267] This manual was written for students who wished to become proficient at playing the organ for worship services. This goal was in keeping with the purpose of DMLC's organ training program. Engel covered all the basics: from proper registration techniques to the proper playing of hymnody. Meyer commented that this volume came about "as a result of his teaching experience."[268] It was published through Dr. Martin Luther College Press and can still be ordered through the Martin Luther College Bookstore and also through Northwestern Publishing House in Milwaukee. Moldenhauer commented that Engel's organ manual is still used at MLC by some of the organ professors. "It is a very practical approach."[269]

. . . in the College Music Classroom

Engel was respected by his students as a classroom teacher. Over the years, he taught at Lutheran grade schools, a Lutheran high school and at two Lutheran colleges. Through various sources that were previously mentioned, we know that he enjoyed teaching music on the college level and spent over two decades of his career teaching at that level. The author was privileged to interview three DMLC students who took music theory and counterpoint classes with Engel. Heller was a student in Engel's Music Theory class. She commented that "he was very skillful in opening up the whole new world of musical composition to his students."[270]

Hirschmann also attended Engel's music theory class and described how Engel often taught the class. Engel would review the previous day's assignment with the class and talk about it. Not only did this activity highlight musical problems, it also allowed the class to hear the musical successes—what chord progressions worked well and which ones really did not. When problems or questions would arise, Engel discussed them with the class. He had his students do some of their work at the chalkboard. He always wanted his students to work through their music theory problems so that they would learn how to compose music according to established music theory rules. He had his students play through the assignments so they could hear what their music sounded like. Aural training benefits all musicians but is especially foundational for composers and improvisers. It is one thing to see music on paper; it is another thing to actually hear what the music really sounds like. "He really made you listen a lot in class to sounds of intervals or chord progressions—things like that."[271] Finally, Hirschmann commented that Engel was always eager to help and encourage his students. Lehman, who also took Music Theory 1 and 2, added that Engel would only go as fast as his students could understand what he was teaching. He provided many examples for his students to analyze and follow. Engel always tried to get homework back to the students quickly so that they could see how they were progressing. He would also point out mistakes, such as parallel fourths and fifths and have his students correct them. They would also have class discussions about theory topics from time to time. And above all, he would take the time to explain things. Engel made sure that every student in his class comprehended the current theory lesson before he moved on to new topics. "He was very thorough and helpful."[272]

> I'll never forget the final for the second theory class. I think there were only five questions, but it took the entire two hours. That was if you worked hard and studied. If you took a two-minute break to clear your mind, you wouldn't get it done. I got an A- on that final exam and I was really happy.[273]

Mr. Dale Witte also attended DMLC in the late 1980s. He studied Music Theory and composition with Engel and took as many theory classes as he could take. These classes included Music Theory 1, 2, 3, and "Counterpoint for Parish Musicians." "As for me, Engel was the person who taught me how to write music."[274] Witte recalls an experience that occurred in one of his music theory classes when he decided to be creative with a composition assignment.

> I remember sitting in one of his Music Theory classes and being given a typical music theory assignment, except I took a chance and didn't complete the assignment like a theory textbook would expect, but I put my own compositional "flair" on it (it was probably an excessive use of arpeggiation). It was his custom to play every student's compositions at the piano in front of the class and then comment on them. His comment on that assignment for me was very complimentary much to the disappointment of the other students in the class. (It seems that many of my classmates struggled with the assignments but I enjoyed them). It was one of the first chances I took on composing music how I felt rather than writing like the "rules" would dictate.[275]

Hirschman commented that Engel would always be willing to help his students outside of class. He would sometimes send his students notes through the campus mail in order to answer their music questions. Engel would often sign his letters "Jim." "I didn't always know how to react. No other professor up there would do that. I, of course, never called him Jim."[276] His students had such respect that they would not think of calling their professor Jim. Things have changed a bit today, but many undergraduate students still refer to their professors using their proper honorifics. "You wouldn't think to call a professor by his first name but it put a friendly face on all his notes. One of his legacies was his kindness to his students and he always had time for his students."[277]

Engel also utilized his music composition students as proofreaders for scores that he intended to send to the publisher for publication. "We were supposed to proofread and look for musical sins and the like."[278] This not only helped Engel catch any musical errors that he had not already noticed, it gave his students experience in music editing and an example of what well-crafted composition looked like.

In summary, Engel was an excellent classroom teacher and was respected by his students and colleagues. He used a variety of techniques to instruct his students and did everything he could to teach them what they needed to know. Engel would go out of his way to help his struggling students when they needed help.

Engel's Influence on Lutheran Church Music

Engel influenced the music of the Lutheran church and the Wisconsin Evangelical Lutheran Synod in particular. He sought to improve the role of church music in the WELS by being a positive example and encouraging musicians to strive at providing the best music possible. Moldenhauer talked about how Engel set a higher standard of music than what was being attained at the time. He talked further about the director whom Engel replaced at Dr. Martin Luther College. "I sang under Meilahn Zahn and I had great respect for him. I enjoyed him as a director, but recordings of our choir under Meilahn Zahn and recordings of Jim Engel's choirs are two different things. He raised the bar."[279]

In the WELS, there were only a few composers who were known outside the church body: people like Bruce Backer, Ronald Schilling and Edward Meyer. Before Engel, there did not seem to be much interest in music publication in the WELS beyond the confines of DMLC. During the 1980s, Northwestern Publishing House started publishing music and one of the first works published was written by Engel.

Engel encouraged Lutheran musicians, students and colleagues alike, to become composers. As Moldenhauer said, Engel was at the same time kind and honest. He would freely give his honest opinion and then give his advice and encouragement. "He was very encouraging to composers that might be active in the hymnal. I remember one of our last conversations that he and I had. We were talking about Evening Prayer, Morning Praise and the seasonal sentences. I had written a set of music for that and had sent it to him for him to review. At one of our last meetings, he talked about that music."[280] Engel encouraged Moldenhauer to continue working on the hymnal project and being an active liturgical composer. He has done this with a passion and has added much to the liturgical corpus used in the WELS. Engel's continual encouragement was a positive influence on composers in the WELS, the LCMS and beyond.

Composition was a daily exercise for Engel. Whether it was writing a short work or constructing only a couple of measures, he made sure that he sat down and put some time into it. "I remember being on the campus here when I was in the high school department and he was in the college department, and he had set a goal for himself that he was going to compose every night—and he did.[281]

A number of his students and colleagues followed his example and have made it a practice to exercise their compositional abilities. This is another fine example of his influence on Lutheran church music through the years.

Engel touched the lives of his students through the years. Some of his students have become well-known musicians and have served in high schools and colleges, while many others have become musical leaders in congregations of the Wisconsin Synod, the Missouri Synod and beyond. Some of the students Engel trained were Donald Busarow, Brenda Glodowski, Glenn Mahnke, Craig Hirschman, Dale Witte, Jeanine Heller, Ken Lehman, Jeffrey Hammes, and others.

Engel had a profound effect on Dale Witte who was in the last generation of Engel students. Back in the 1970s, Witte lived in East Troy, Wisconsin and was the son of the pastor there. The DMLC College Choir, under the direction of Engel, came to St. Paul's Lutheran Church in East Troy to sing for their Easter service. It was part of their annual spring choir tour during that year. Witte recalls:

> I remember waiting at the church door watching for the big busses to roll into our dusty parking lot. It was the custom that the children of each congregation would sing one song with them during the service or concert. I think it was the Sunday School children who learned a song to sing with the College Choir that Easter, but what sticks out in my memory was the cold I had that Easter. It was the

kind of cold that every time I took a deep breath (like the kind you should take when singing) I had to cough. Well, being one of the youngest children in the Sunday School choir, I remember standing in the very front row of children, in the front of the whole church, standing in front of all the college students, right in the middle of the front row, watching Engel for my cue to come in. But every time I took a breath, I coughed. And every time I coughed, Engel looked at me. So my first singing debut for Engel was an auspicious one because I think he spent more time looking at this poor, sick, little boy in the front row of the Sunday School wondering if he was alright than he was concerned about the College Choir and how they sounded during that song on Easter Sunday morning.[282]

Eventually Witte went to college at DMLC and had Engel as a music theory and composition teacher. He learned much from Engel and later became a well-known composer in his own right within the WELS. Witte recalls that after Engel's death, he prayed that the Lord would give him the ability to take up Engel's mantle:

I knew that God had blessed Engel with being a gifted church musician and composer, but as I looked around with the limited view of the WELS that I knew at that time, I didn't see anyone else who could take up the work of composing for the Church as Engel had done. So I prayed that if it was God's will, that He allow me to be just such a composer and musician for His church as Engel was. God has answered that prayer for me by allowing me to write liturgical settings, choral music, and keyboard music for use in Lutheran worship.[283]

Over the years, Witte has directed church choirs, played the organ and directed the choir at Winnebago Lutheran Academy. He has, in turn, influenced many young students and guided them into a life of music. "I can only pray that God continues to answer my prayer all of my life so I can always make music to the Lord with all my heart like I saw Engel do when I was in college."[284]

Engel also cared about his students' futures and success. The author talked with a number of Engel's former students and heard the same high praise. Glodowski commented that when Engel found out that she was planning on attending the University of Wisconsin at Stevens Point, he gave her advice and helped her prepare for her scholarship audition. Due in part to Engel's extra effort, Glodowski earned her scholarship, completed her course of study and graduated. She also credits Engel as a key influence on her going into the career of a high school music teacher.[285] Glodowski goes on to say the following about his influence on her choice of profession:

> I remember what a strong impression he made on me as a teen in his choir. That's a big piece right there. I recall thinking, I already knew that music was an awesome thing, but if it can cause this grown man to stop in his tracks and feel compelled to share his musical insight with us because of his passion for it, there must be something about the music that only a choral director can experience. It's one thing to sing in the choir, but to be the choral director up-front, he must have a different experience with the music. He just drove me to find out what that was.[286]

Glodowski relayed another story about Engel that occurred when she was the director of the choirs at West Lutheran High School, located in Plymouth, Minnesota, a suburb of the Twin Cities. This story that she relays to us was one of those profound and meaningful experiences in her career. While she does not recall the exact year, the National Choral Festival was being hosted by DMLC that year. The National Choral Festival is a gathering of WELS Lutheran high school choirs from around the country. They perform a pops concert and also a sacred concert. Many students who have gone to these events have found them to be "top-of-the-mountain" experiences. Attending a National Choral Festival was something that has made a profound and meaningful impact upon many who have participated in them. This particular choral festival was held only a few years before Engel's death. In the year of the festival, Glodowski told her students about how excited she was about taking them to this choral festival. She remembers telling her students about Engel and the piece that he specially composed for the choral festival. She said, "Professor Engel wrote a song for the festival and he's going to direct it. He was my high school director, and he's the reason that I am doing what I am doing today, so this is a very cool thing."[287] She recalls asking if she could stay with the Engels while she was in New Ulm for the concert. Her request was granted, so she was able to stay with them. Glodowski paints the following scene:

> One night we were talking and I had mentioned something about that I had done some arranging on one of the pieces or something like that. And we talked a little bit about writing music and he started talking to me like I was a peer, not like I was a former student. And he encouraged me and he said that to write, you must write. And that's all that had to be said. All of the sudden, he was pulling out all of his manuscripts, you know, some half done, some that he had just got back from the publisher, and he spread that all out on the table and we sat next to each other at the table and looked through this music. He was talking to me about the process, and it just blew me away. Like I just mentioned earlier, he was talking to me like I was a peer, and that just meant the world to me.[288]

This was a special experience for Glodowski. She appreciated that Engel was willing to again share his passion for music with her again. This time it was his passion for music composition.

There is a common feeling among many of the people with whom the author talked that we are still feeling the effects of Engel's work within the Wisconsin Synod to this day. We can see it in his music and can feel it in the lives and work of his former students. This legacy will continue to be felt for years to come.

Engel's Music

In addition to his teaching career, Engel became known as a composer of Lutheran church music. He created well-crafted works that were intended to fulfill specific musical roles in worship services and concerts alike. Engel wrote choral works for use with the choirs he directed. Some of them were for his male choirs while many others were for mixed choirs.

Engel was known for writing organ works for his students. A few of these works were written for teaching purposes while the majority of them were written for students as introductions for hymns used for DMLC's chapel services. He wrote works for himself which he played at St. John in Sleepy Eye. Engel also wrote larger organ and choral works for major campus concerts and organ dedication services. His music ranged from simple, finely written compositions to complex works requiring solid performance technique from the organist, choir and other musicians.

Engel was very practical about his music. He generally wrote music in such a way that it could be used in the average parish. As is already known, he had an intimate knowledge of the type of music needed in the parish and also knew the average ability of his students. Engel did not write incidental music. It was music that served a purpose and was carefully constructed to perform that task. As Moldenhauer commented, Engel's music was never mediocre. "I always had the sense that he wanted things that were accessible by a good number of folks."[289] This is not to say that Engel did not write complex music but he tended to focus much of his work towards his students and parish musicians. Engel did not limit himself to harmonic styles of the past but also used some 20th-century harmonies in his music. Yet such harmonies were used sparingly in order to add harmonic interest to his music but not offend the sensibilities of parishioners. Moldenhauer comments: "He never went over the edge for me—never got over to the atonal style—way over."[290]

Moldenhauer commented that Engel brought a rhythmic vitality to his choral compositions. "He brought something fresh, rhythmically to choral composition that we hadn't seen in our circles before. It was new and fresh."[291] This, along with his use of harmony, made his music exciting while bringing to bear centuries of music history on his music.

Engel employed a wide variety of musical styles in his compositions. Moldenhauer commented: "You could tell that he was a student of history, the way he employed the musical styles from the ages."[292] When the author talked with Hirschmann, he recalled that Engel also had a love for the music of neo-classicist composers such as Hindemith and Pepping. He also admired the works of Wilbur Held and Theodore Beck. Engel not only studied their writing styles but also suggested that his students should emulate them as well.[293] The goal was to write unique music while building upon the styles of these other well-known church composers. "I don't think he was trying to be a copycat but he admired that particular type of writing."[294] These composers should be studied and their work should be seen as models of what quality church music composition should be.

When looking at Engel's advanced works, a person cannot help but see how his vast knowledge of musical style throughout history shines forth. His *Variations on In Dulci Jubilo* is a prime example of this. Engel used his knowledge of historical musical styles to create a fine partita that is on one hand, a cohesive unit, and on the other hand, varied in style. Compositional styles included within sections of this work include: Baroque, French Romantic, and 20th-century. It was written in honor of the dedication of the Schlicker organ at Wisconsin Lutheran College. That instrument was dedicated in September of 1989. The author had the privilege of attending that event and hearing this partita played in concert for the first time. It was a sad fact that the composer was not able to be there to hear it played but his wife and other members of his family were in attendance. The partita was published in 1989 by Concordia Publishing House. Unfortunately, this beautiful piece is no longer in print.

Engel wrote many of his organ works while teaching at Dr. Martin Luther College. Dr. Edward Meyer commented on some of Engel's organ compositions. Meyer worked very closely with Engel on a number of organ composition projects and had much to say about Engel's compositional work.

The *Eleven Chorale Preludes for Organ* was published through Dr. Martin Luther College. The first edition of this work was produced using a manuscript style. "It's in his own hand script" said Meyer. "[H]e wrote them for the beginning organ student, as the foreword said," and used them as part of his organ teaching. "I remember when we put it together, I was chairman, and very much interested in the project."[295] The second edition was published in 1981 and was scored on a music typewriter. In the original edition, the scores were organized by English text titles. However, in the 1981 edition, the scores were organized by German tune titles. Meyer commented that this compilation of chorale preludes was "very popular" with DMLC's students and music faculty. "We often discussed the success of this, the interest that teachers had and how accessible as it was to beginning students."[296] After Engel's death, a version of this set was published by MorningStar Music Publishers in 1993. It was titled *9 Easy Chorale Preludes for the Christmas Season* and was published without the two preludes on "Lord, to Thee I Make Confession."

The *Organ Preludes for the Passion Season* was originally published through Dr. Martin Luther College in 1983. It was later republished as *9 Easy Chorale Preludes for Lent* by MorningStar in 1994. It is noteworthy to mention that the prelude on "The Royal Banners Forward Go" [VEXILLA REGIS] was not published in the new MorningStar edition.

The *Centennial Organ Collection*[297] was composed and collected in 1983 in order for it to be ready for the centennial of Dr. Martin Luther College. A similar choral book was also compiled at that time. Meyer stated "[B]eing chairman [of the music department], I served as the committee chairman myself. I did the work myself. I invited anyone on the staff to submit compositions, and the reason being is that I felt that at 100 years we ought to have a collection of organ music to show future generations where we were and what we were doing at that time."[298] Engel contributed five works to the collection.

He chose the tunes that he wanted to set and submit. Meyer did not edit these works but rather accepted them "as is" and organized them into the Centennial Collection. It is a fine collection of music and very representative of the fine composing work that was being done on campus at that time.[299]

The *Concordia Hymn Prelude Series* was a landmark collection of organ music for the Lutheran worship service. This resource provided preludes and hymn introduction for the hymns found in the following hymnals: *The Lutheran Hymnal (1941)*, *Lutheran Book of Worship (1978)* and *Lutheran Worship (1982)*. The collection spans the liturgical church year including hymns used in the non-festival half. The series comprises forty-two volumes and includes 720 hymn preludes. The first six volumes of this collection were published in 1982 and the final volumes were published in 1986. The composers represented in this collection are a "Who's Who" of Lutheran organ composition. Composers who are represented include: Jan Bender (1909-1994), Paul Bouman (1918-2019), Donald Busarow (1934-2011), John Eggert (b.1946), James Engel (1925-1989), Hugo Gehrke (1912-1992), Wilber Held 1914-2015), Kenneth Kosche (b. 1947), Austin Lovelace (1919-2010), Walter Pelz (b. 1926), Carl Schalk (b. 1929), and Ronald Shilling (b.1941), Dr. Herbert Gotsch began as the editor for the series but he died on March 8, 1984. Dr. Richard Hillert succeeded Gotsch as editor and completed the last twelve volumes of this collection.[300]

Engel contributed twenty-three compositions to this collection. The first volumes focused on Advent and Christmas. "He was quite pleased to be part of the group of composers who contributed to the Hymn Prelude Series. He often talked about them."[301]

"Preludes in the series were supposed to be for organists who had limited to average ability."[302] One can expect limited pedal lines in the early volumes of this collection. This ideal fit well into the works that Engel was composing for his students. Meyer comments that the music Engel contributed to the collection adhered to those ideals. Engel's work for his students was well-crafted and accessible to his students. These pieces are perfect for the busy parish musician who does not have as much time to practice and perfect complicated service music.

Meyer stated that as more of the volumes came out, the music tended to get more difficult and not as easily accessible to the average organist. Meyer further commented that Engel was not pleased with this development since it went against what he felt to be the primary goals of the collection. "They did get a little harder, particularly the Easter ones, if you take a look at some of those. There are some very difficult ones in there."[303] The Concordia Series filled a need in Lutheran parishes for accessible service music for the organ and Engel was honored to be a part of it.

Meyer told an interesting story regarding the next piece, *A Little Chaconne on a Lenten Hymn*:

> [Engel] came into my office one day, and he said one word as he put some pages on my desk. And he said "Here," had a gentle smile on his face, and then raced out. I said, "OK, Good morning, Jim." Well, when I saw what it was, I realized it was the manuscript form of this [piece], and I said "Oh, that's really very interesting." And it wasn't until later on that I noticed that there was a dedication to me. So that's how it started, and I had the manuscript, the handwritten copy of it.[304]

This composition, as Wegner pointed out, is modeled after the "Chaconne in F-Major" by Henry Purcell. Engel purposefully patterned his piece after this great work and melded it with the hymn "Stricken, Smitten, and Afflicted."[305] Meyer recalls playing a dedication recital where he featured music that had been written by composers from the Wisconsin Synod. "I invited several other composers throughout synod to give me some manuscripts."[306] This was the piece that he chose to represent Engel at that concert. The playing of this work was meant as a tribute since Engel was no longer living at that time.[307]

Northwestern Publishing House published two collections of preludes that Engel had written. They were titled the *Nineteen Hymn Introductions for the Organ* and the *Twenty Hymn Introductions for the Organ*. They were published at a time when Northwestern was just getting back into the music publishing business after a hiatus of many years. A person might notice that the first volume has nineteen hymn introductions and the second volume has twenty hymn introductions. One can surmise that the third volume, had it been published, would have been twenty-one, and so forth. This was not by happenstance but was based on what Jan Bender had previously done with his intonation volumes (published by CPH). Meyer mentioned that Engel had said: "Well, if Jan Bender could do it, then I'm going to do it too." He kind of chuckled about that and said 'I'm going to do the same thing.'"[308]

These hymn introductions were intended for the Lutheran parish organist. Meyer recalled that many of these intonations were written for Sunday worship at St. John, Sleepy Eye, Minnesota. It was his feeling that Engel wrote a number of these intonations on short notice for use in his upcoming Sunday worship services. They are certainly well-crafted and very accessible to the busy church musician/school teacher.[309] Meyer recalls reading a review regarding these volumes. The reviewer, who was not familiar with the music of the Wisconsin Synod, questioned "whether people actually sing these quaint tunes."[310] Engel responded to the reviewer by telling him that these hymns are the "bread and butter" of Lutheran hymnody and were valuable to Lutheran parishes. Meyer recalled that Engel found it funny and was able to chuckle about it. Meyer also commented that it was his belief that Engel would have published more volumes in this series had he lived longer.[311]

While the author has focused on Engel's organ music, Engel also wrote a large portion of his work throughout his career for his choirs. He was continually writing and reworking choral pieces for his choirs to sing.[312] Following is information about some of Engel's choral works.

Wegner spoke about Engel's "From Heaven Above to Earth I Come." It is a concertato for choir, organ, three trumpets and congregation. He noted the dedication at the top of the first page which reads: "To Mr. Richard Wegner and the choirs of Immanuel Lutheran Church, Baltimore, Maryland."[313] There are ten stanzas in this concertato using a variety of vocal and instrumental forces, from a soloist accompanied by an 8' flute on the organ, to SATB choir, and congregation with a bold organ accompaniment and three trumpets. This piece was published in 1981 by Augsburg Publishing House. (See Appendix D—cover from Richard Wegner's score of *From Heaven Above*.)

One of the more interesting collaborative projects that Engel and Meyer embarked upon was the *Hymn Settings*. These choral settings of selected hymns and were published in two volumes. Volume One was published in 1981 and Volume Two was published in 1987. Meyer had been very interested in involving Engel because he wrote quality music. "I felt that there was a real need for us to tap into that ability and his creative genius and make it available to our [WELS] constituency."[314] Engel took interest in the project and a partnership was born.

The two collections of *Hymn Settings* were written for the parish teacher/music director as a source of music for school children to sing. "I had a theory at that particular time that our teachers in our schools, faced with various situations and different schools from the small to the large, often didn't have settings of the hymns from the hymnal available to them."[315] While school choirs were the primary focus of these volumes, they could easily be used by small parish choirs who had limited vocal resources but had an interest in enriching their worship services.

Each volume contained choral arrangements based on twelve hymns. Engel composed on six hymn tunes and Meyer composed on six more. He commented that each hymn tune would have at least five settings. They agreed on guidelines for the volumes and followed them. "[W]e always had a minimum of five or six setting, starting with unison, two-part homophonic, two-part contrapuntal, three-part, and then the last one was to be an SAB setting for changing voice because [the collection] was marketed for the schools."[316] Meyer commented that they tested many of these works in DMLC chapel services before they published them. They were sometimes sung by the College Chorale and other times sung by students who were enrolled in the music teaching course.[317]

After they were composed, Meyer compiled them into the volumes now in print. He did the engraving, marketing and kept track of all the sales. These duties included mailing copies out to customers and billing for these items. "We sold master sheets and people ran off what they wanted."[318] Meyer holds the copyright for them. "We simply had an agreement. The two of us said that if there would be any proceeds, we would divide them 50/50, and we did that until and after he passed away. Mrs. Engel continued to receive a yearly check until there were no more sales. Then the excess copies were destroyed."[519]

The first volume sold well and was widely used within the Wisconsin Synod. However, Meyer commented that by the time the second volume came out, many non-hymnal-based resources were becoming popular in our Christian schools and parishes. The demand for this type of resource simply started to wane.[320]

"I Walk with Angels" is one of Engel's signature compositions. Everyone that the author has interviewed has counted this work as his most noteworthy piece. Wegner specifically stated that he counted *I Walk with Angels* as Engel's finest piece.[321] A recording of this work can be found on Wegner's CD (copyrighted in 1995) titled: *Organ Music from Immanuel. I Walk with Angels* was recorded by the Immanuel Choir along with strings and organ.[322] In the preface to *I Walk with Angels*, it was noted that this work was composed "for the January 1976 graduation service in the chapel at Dr. Martin Luther College, New Ulm, Minnesota." The dedication at the top of the score reads: "To my dear wife, Norma."[323] When the author talked with Mrs. Engel and her daughters, Joan Mueller and Mary Geis, it was obvious that this piece was dear to all of them.

This little cantata consists of four parts: Sinfonia, Recitative, Aria, and Chorale. It reminded the author of the classical construction found in the cantatas of J. S. Bach. The piece is scored for choir, organ, cello and two oboes. In the preface to this work, it is noted that "Solo or ensemble strings may be substituted for the oboe parts." The chorale is "Der lieben Sonne Licht und Pracht." In English we sing the hymn text, "I Walk in Danger All the Way," and this chorale is found in many Lutheran hymnals. The title for this cantata actually comes from the fourth stanza of the hymn. The text from stanzas four and six is used in parts three and four of this cantata. He used a slightly varied text for the third line of the chorale, but when considering the text Engel used, it seems to the author to be a fitting textual alternative to the text found in *The Lutheran Hymnal*: "With Christ, my Savior guide, and angel hosts beside."

I Walk with Angels was published in 1978 by Chantry Press.[324] Engel had often commented to Meyer that the owner of that press was often unpredictable in regard to the timetable of when the music would be completed and ready for publication. [The owner was a busy Lutheran pastor—Ed.] However his company's work was excellent. "[He] did beautiful, beautiful work. Outstanding engraving. At this point we didn't have computers that could do this yet. It all had to be done by hand."[325]

The faculty and print shop of Dr. Martin Luther College did a lot of publishing through the years. In the late 1970s and early 1980s, manuscripts were handwritten and printed, but by 1983, the college purchased a music writer. A music writer was basically a typewriter that typed music. "It was built on the frame of a real typewriter, but instead of getting letters out of it, you got the notes." The process could be tedious to use because it required perfect alignment in order to type notes on the page with the proper placement. "You had to take the roller and if it was an "E," you'd put it here and type a quarter note, and if it was an "F," you'd roll it up a little bit further. So each note had to be put in one at a time."[326] The quality of music writer manuscripts for the publication of music was a vast improvement over the neatest hand-written copies that were previously available. So much work was being done with this tool that a second music writer was purchased. The one drawback that was mentioned was that this machine required special ribbons. As one can imagine, those that used the music writer went through many ribbons and they were more expensive than regular typewriter ribbons. Yet the benefits of the music writer outweighed the cost of the ribbons.

To the composer of today, the music writer may seem like a crude tool. Composers now have powerful computers, expert music writing software and printers that can produce quality physical output. However, the first music writing computers did not become available until the late 1980s. The music writer was the best technology available to Engel at that time for a small college press in the music publishing business. Meyer commented that Engel was himself proficient on the music writer.[327] This skill-set goes hand-in-hand with his interest in and investigation of the new computer technology for music that developed later.

The author has often wondered how much more music Engel would have written and published with the technology that we have today. We now have the ability to play music into the computer, listen to it, edit it and output the result to a printer. The results from a high quality printer can look almost as good as the output from a publishing company. Engel saw the beginning of this in the late 1980s and comprehended how this new technology would change the world of music publishing.

Many composers increase their composing output after they retire from their professional careers. There is generally more time available to devote to composition. Many of the people the author talked with have speculated about what he would have written had he lived longer. If his posthumous pieces are any indication, we would have seen much more music written at the height of Engel's musical skill. He wrote for the average church musician but his music was not average. One can speculate that with more time available in retirement, Engel most likely would have written more works similar in scope to his *Variations on In Dulci Jubilo* for Organ, or his *I Walk with Angels* for choir. As Hirschmann commented, "I still can not help but think there was a lot of publishing left in him, but for whatever the reason, the Lord called him home at that time."[328]

Engel's works were published by a variety of publishing houses through the years. One of these publishers was MorningStar Music Publishers, currently located in Fenton, Missouri. MorningStar was founded by Rodney Schrank, the former director of music publications at Concordia Publishing House. Engel and Schrank had been friends for many years.[329] When Engel died, Schrank "sought and received Norma Engel's permission to sort through all of Jim's manuscripts seeking material for posthumous publication."[330] Mrs. Engel gave permission, and a number of works were sent down to Missouri for publication. "MorningStar was ready to publish anything that he wrote."[331] One of his works, "My Song Is Love Unknown," was slightly incomplete at Engel's death. Most of it was set but there was an "alternate reading" in stanza four as stated in the score. It is uncertain which version Engel would have used for his final score. Both versions are printed in the score, and it is up to the director to decide which "reading" to perform. The author was able to identify ten of Engel's works which MorningStar published posthumously.

Conclusion

Life is a journey from cradle to grave. James and Norma Engel, along with their eldest daughter, Kathy, now walk with the angels in heaven. In terms of this earthly existence, we are remembered by the people who loved us, the people whose lives we have touched, and those tangible things we have left behind. Engel will be remembered for his music and by the people who sing and play that music. He will also be remembered by his many students who carry on his legacy of music and service to God. Finally, he will be remembered by his family and friends, those who continue to sojourn on this earth, awaiting God's call to join James and Norma Engel in their walk with angels in the glory of heaven.

Endnotes

1. Engel was baptized on April 12, 1925, at Jerusalem Evangelical Church in Milwaukee, Wisconsin by Pastor H. Gieschen. (James Engel's Funeral Bulletin.) Obituary.

2. C. T. Aufdemberge, *Christian Worship: Handbook* (Milwaukee, WI: Northwestern, 1997), 699.

3. Engel's Godmother, Anna, can be remembered today for some of her hymns found in a variety of Lutheran hymnals. In *Christian Worship: A Lutheran Hymnal*, we find the hymn "Rise, Arise"/#30. She is also known for her translations of German hymns. "This night a wondrous revelation" is a prime example of her translation work and is found in a number of Lutheran hymnals. In 1928, some of her hymns appeared in *The Northwestern Lutheran*, the official journal of the Wisconsin Evangelical Lutheran Synod "Twenty-three of her hymns were included in the 1925 Augustana Synod's *The Hymnal*." During her life, Anna wrote about 400 hymn texts and over 600 poems. Aufdemberge, *Christian Worship: Handbook*, 745-746. The Center for Church music published in 2018 *Anna B. Hoppe: Her Life and Hymnody*, written by Elisabeth Joy Urtel.

4. Norma Engel, interview by author, Appleton, WI, June 20, 2005.

5. Mary Geis, June 2, 2008, email message to author.

6. Geis email.

7. Norma Engel interview.

8. Wegner interview.

9. Norma Engel interview.

10. *Bethlehem Lutheran School History*, (Milwaukee, WI: The school, 1984), 10.

11. Janet Engel, April 5, 2007, letter to author.

12. Ibid.

13. Richard Wegner, interview by author, Baltimore, MD, May 22, 2008.

14. Ibid.

15. Ibid.

16. Lutheran High School was founded in 1903 and has the distinction of being one of the first Lutheran high schools in the United. States.

17. Carol Krause, "History of Wisconsin Lutheran High School," Wisconsin Lutheran High School, http://www.wlhs.org/4history.htm [accessed March 19, 2009].

[18] Wegner interview.

[19] Norma Engel interview.

[20] Wegner interview.

[21] Ibid.

[22] The organ was recently rebuilt (in 2006-2008), restored and enhanced by the Schantz organ company of Orrville, Ohio, and is back in working order. Special care was taken to assure that the E.M. Skinner pipe voicing and sound were retained and, in some cases, restored. Thus, the restored organ is now very much the instrument that Engel and Wegner played back in 1945-46. Schantz Organ Company, http://www.schantzorgan.com/RecentDetail.cfm?yJob=2274 [accessed March 19, 2009].

[23] Wegner interview.

[24] Ibid.

[25] Ibid.

[26] John H. Hallmann, "First Zion Evangelical Lutheran Church", http://pages.prodigy.net/johnhhallmann/firstzionchi.htm [accessed June 11, 2010].

[27] Norma Engel interview.

[28] Wegner interview.

[29] Mary Geis, interview by author, Baltimore, MD, May 22, 2008.

[30] Norma Engel interview.

[31] (James Engel's Funeral Bulletin.) Obituary.

[32] Wegner, Geis interview.

[33] Wegner interview.

[34] Ibid.

[35] Ibid.

[36] Ibid.

[37] Richard Wegner, phone interview by author, March 10, 2010.

[38] Gehrke later moved back to Milwaukee in the mid-1970s and taught music at Concordia College in Milwaukee.

[39] Lutheran A Capella Choir of Milwaukee, "Choir history," Lutheran A Capella Choir, http://www.lutheranacapella.org/choir_history.htm [accessed April 1, 2009].

[40] Suzanne Eggold, interview by author, Grafton, WI, November 14, 2009.

[41] Eggold interview.

[42] Aufdemberge, Christian Worship: Handbook, 699.

[43] Eggold interview.

[44] Ibid.

[45] Wegner phone interview.

[46] Fred Bartel, June 3, 2006, email message to author.

[47] Meyer interview.

[48] Wegner interview.

[49] Meyer interview.

[50] Aufdemberge, *Christian Worship: Handbook*, 699.

[51] Wegner interview.

[52] Donald Busarow, June 5, 2006, email message to author.

[53] Ibid.

[54] Arthur Preuss, interview by author, Racine, WI, June 15, 2007.

[55] Dorothy Croll, interview by author, Baltimore, MD, May 22, 2008.

[56] According to Grant Malme, a highly regarded professor from Racine College of Music, the college was originally affiliated as "a branch of the Milwaukee Musical College." Soon after Malme joined the faculty, Racine College of Music became an independent institution. The school is no longer in existence. Grant Malme, June 16, 2007, letter to author.

[57] Ibid.

[58] Norma Engel interview.

[59] Malme letter.

[60] "Masters give duo-piano recital." *Concordia Courier*. 28, no. 2 (March 21, 1960):3.

[61] Marci Tenuta, "Talk of the town: Piano teacher to receive a big thank-you for his years of compassionate instruction," *Racine Journal Times*. May 2, 2007.

[62] Croll interview.

[63] Wegner interview.

[64] Geis email.

[65] Eldon Balko, March 28, 2007, email message to author.

[66] Concordia College centennial jubilee, 1881-1981 (Mequon WI: The college, 1984), 29.

[67] Ibid.

[68] Ibid, 31.

[69] Ibid, 34.

[70] Balko email, March 28, 2007.

[71] Croll interview.

[72] Wegner interview.

[73] Wegner interview.

[74] Rodney Gehrke, July 13, 2007, email message to the author.

[75] Gehrke email.

[76] "Classical organ planned for chapel." *Concordia Courier* 30, no. 1 (January 17, 1962):4.

[77] Glenn Mahnke, January 21, 2008, email message to author.

[78] Ibid.

[79] Ibid.

[80] Ibid.

[81] Ibid.

[82] "Concordia chapel to get new organ." *Concordia Courier* 30, no. 4 (September 28, 1961):4.

[83] James Burmeister, interview by author, Glendale, WI, April 25, 2007.

[84] Dedicatory organ recital folder, Memorial Lutheran Church, Glendale, WI.

[85] Glenn Mahnke, January 23, 2008, email message to author.

[86] "New organ for chapel dedicated." *Concordia Courier* 31, no. 5 (November 30, 1963):1.

[87] "Dedicatory recital." *Concordia Courier* 32, no. 1 (February 28, 1964):3.

[88] Mahnke email, January 21, 2008.

[89] Burmeister interview.

[90] Ibid.

[91] Ibid.

[92] Ibid.

[93] Ibid.

[94] Balko email, March 28, 2007.

[95] Mahnke email, January 21, 2008.

[96] Balko email, March 28, 2007.

[97] Eldon Balko, March 26, 2007, email message to author.

[98] Balko email, March 28, 2007.

[99] *Concordia College Centennial Jubilee*, 32.

[100] Ibid., 35-36.

[101] Balko email, March 28, 2007.

[102] Geis email.

[103] Mahnke email, January 23, 2008.

[104] Ibid.

[105] Ibid.

[106] Geis email.

[107] Balko email, March 28, 2007.

[108] Mahnke email, January 21, 2008.

[109] Geis email.

[110] Ibid.

[111] Dorothy Piel, March 31, 2008, email message to author.

[112] *Immanuel 100th Anniversary*. (Milwaukee, WI: Immanuel Lutheran Church, 1966), 17.

[113] Geis email.

[114] Ibid.

[115] Ibid.

[116] Stanton Peters, December 31, 2007, letter to the author.

[117] The Organ Reform Movement (also commonly known as the Orgelbewegung) was a movement concerned with the historical performance of organ music on instruments built upon historical designs. The movement was a reaction to Romantic and Orchestral organs that were commonly built in the earth 20th century.

[118] Peters letter.

[119] Ibid.

120 Ibid.

121 Ibid.

122 Ibid.

123 Jeffrey Hammes, September 7, 2007, email message to author.

124 Geis email.

125 Piel email.

126 Ibid.

127 Ibid.

128 Ibid.

129 Preuss interview.

130 Edward Meyer, interview by the author, Stillwater, MN, August 31, 2007.

131 Norma Engel interview.

132 Mahnke email, January 21, 2008.

133 Norma Engel interview.

134 Northern Wisconsin District, WELS, *Northward in Christ: a history of the Northern Wisconsin District of the Wisconsin Synod Evangelical Lutheran Synod* (S.1.: Northern Wisconsin District, WELS, 2000), 164-168.

135 Norma Engel interview.

136 Meyer interview.

137 Brenda Glodowski, phone interview by author, September 5, 2006.

138 Ibid.

139 Norma Engel interview.

140 Joan Mueller, interview by author, Appleton, WI, June 20, 2005.

141 Norma Engel interview.

142 Mueller interview.

143 Glodowski phone interview.

144 Geis email.

145 Aufdemberge, *Christian Worship: Handbook*, 700.

146 Norma Engel interview.

147 Ronald Ash, interview by author, Appleton, WI, June 17, 2007.

148 *Rejoice! What great things God has done for us: 125th anniversary of St. Peter Ev. Lutheran Church* (Freedom, WI.: The church, 1993), 6-7.

149 Ash interview.

150 Norma Engel interview.

151 Ibid.

152 Ibid.

153 Mueller interview.

154 Norma Engel interview.

155 Ibid.

156 Geis email.

157 Meyer interview.

158 Ibid.

159 Ibid.

160 Craig Hirschmann, interview by author, Milwaukee, WI, June 27, 2006.

161 Ibid.

162 Meyer interview.

163 "Who's new on campus." *DMLC Messenger* 66, no. 1 (October 10, 1975): 1.

164 Meyer interview.

165 Hirschmann interview.

166 Ibid.

167 Meyer interview.

168 Ibid.

169 Ibid.

170 "College Choir goes on tour." *DMLC Messenger* 70, no. 5:1.

171 "DMLC choir tour recap." *DMLC Messenger* 70, no. 6:3.

172 Meyer interview.

173 Ibid.

174 Ibid.

175 Ibid.

176 Ibid.

177 Ibid.

178 Ibid.

179 Wegner interview.

180 Ibid.

181 Norma Engel interview.

182 Mueller interview.

183 Norma Engel interview.

184 Hirschmann interview.

185 Ibid.

186 Hirschmann interview.

187 Norma Engel interview.

188 Ibid.

189 Hirschmann interview.

190 Ibid.

191 Ibid.

192 William H. Braun and Victor H. Prange, eds., *Not unto Us: a Celebration of the Ministry of Kurt J. Eggert* (Milwaukee, WI: Northwestern, 2001), 192.

193 Victor Prange, June 9, 2009, email message to author.

194 Braun and Prange, *Not unto Us*, 187.

195 Moldenhauer interview.

196 Prange interview.

197 Braun and Prange, *Not unto Us*, 192.

[198] Ibid.
[199] Ibid.
[200] Norma Engel interview.
[201] Moldernhauer interview.
[202] Ibid.
[203] Ibid.
[204] Ibid.
[205] Ibid.
[206] Ibid.
[207] Ibid.
[208] Hirschmann interview.
[209] Wegner interview.
[210] Geis email.
[211] Ibid.
[212] Ibid.
[213] Dale Witte, August 16, 2006, email message to author.
[214] Geis email.
[215] Ibid.
[216] Ibid.
[217] Ibid.
[218] Ibid.
[219] Ibid.
[220] Ibid.
[221] Ibid.
[222] Ibid.
[223] Ibid.
[224] Jeanine Heller, January 1, 2008, email message to author.
[225] Heller email.
[226] Hirschmann interview.
[227] Heller email.
[228] Mahnke email, January 21, 2008.
[229] Balko email, March 28, 2007.
[230] Ibid.
[231] Moldenhauer interview.
[232] Meyer interview.
[233] Ibid.
[234] Balko email, March 28, 2007.
[235] Ibid.
[236] Glodowski phone interview.
[237] Mueller interview.
[238] Norma Engel interview.

[239] Mahnke email, January 23, 2008.

[240] Heller email.

[241] Hammes later co-founded an organ building company with Gary Foxe. There are a number of fine organs in the southeastern Wisconsin area which were built by the Hammes-Foxe firm.

[242] Jeffrey P. Hammes, September 7, 2007, email message to author.

[243] Ibid.

[244] Mahnke email, January 23, 2008.

[245] Heller email.

[246] Ibid.

[247] Ibid.

[248] Ibid.

[249] Kenneth Lehman, interview by author, La Crosse, Wisconsin, December 27, 2006.

[250] Hirschmann interview.

[251] Ibid.

[252] Ibid.

[253] Ibid.

[254] Ibid.

[255] Ibid.

[256] Ibid.

[257] Ibid.

[258] Ibid.

[259] Lehman interview.

[260] Heller email.

[261] Hirschmann interview.

[262] Ibid.

[263] Ibid.

[264] Ibid.

[265] Mahnke email, January 21, 2008.

[266] Balko email, March 28, 2007.

[267] James Engel, *A Manual for the Beginning Church Organist.* (New Ulm, MN.: DMLC Press, n.d.), Title page.

[268] Meyer interview.

[269] Moldenhauer interview.

[270] Heller email.

[271] Hirschmann interview.

[272] Lehman interview.

[273] Ibid.

[274] Witte email.

[275] Ibid.

[276] Hirschmann interview.

277 Ibid.

278 Ibid.

279 Moldenhauer interview.

280 Ibid.

281 Ibid.

282 Witte email.

283 Ibid.

284 Ibid.

285 Glodowski phone interview.

286 Ibid.

287 Ibid.

288 Ibid.

289 Moldenhauer interview.

290 Ibid.

291 Ibid.

292 Ibid.

293 Hirschmann interview.

294 Ibid.

295 Meyer interview.

296 Ibid.

297 Copies of this collection can be purchased through Northwestern Publishing House in Milwaukee, Wisconsin and the Martin Luther College Bookstore in New Ulm, Minnesota.

298 Meyer interview.

299 Ibid.

300 *The Concordia Hymn Preludes Series Index* (St. Louis, MO: Concordia, 1986), 6.

301 Meyer interview.

302 Ibid.

303 Ibid.

304 Ibid.

305 Wegner interview.

306 Meyer interview.

307 Ibid.

308 Ibid.

309 Ibid.

310 Ibid.

311 Ibid.

312 Heller email.

313 Wegner interview.

314 Meyer interview.

[315] Ibid.

[316] Ibid.

[317] Ibid.

[318] Ibid.

[319] Ibid.

[320] Ibid.

[321] Wegner interview.

[322] Ibid.

[323] James Engel, *I Walk with Angels* (Springfield, OH: Chantry Music Press, 1978), 3.

[324] Copies of *I Walk with Angels* can still be obtained through the Augsburg Fortress Press copyright office.

[325] Meyer interview.

[326] Ibid.

[327] Ibid.

[328] Hirschmann interview.

[329] Norma Engel interview.

[330] Mahnke email, January 21, 2008.

[331] Norma Engel interview.

Catalog of Engel's Music

The following section is a music catalog of Engel's works including both published and unpublished material. The author included as many of Engel's works as he could find. The author believes that there are other unpublished works unknown to him that are held by students and other individuals. The titles of the works included here are cataloged chronologically by date using the Anglo-American Cataloging Rules format, Second Edition (AACR2). A second brief catalog listing titles by genre follows the first catalog (p. 120ff).

Chronological Order

Works completed during James Engel's years at St. John Lutheran Church in Racine, WI.

Two chorale preludes / James Engel Saint Louis, Mo. : Concordia, 1949. 4 p. of music ; 32 cm. Contents:
> O God, Thou Faithful God
> Kyrie, God Father in Heaven Above

Works completed during James Engel's years at Concordia College in Milwaukee, WI.

Silent night [Manuscript] : verse two / James Engel. 1 score (1 p.)
> Notes: SATB a cappella.

> Manuscript found in the choral files at Gospel Evangelical Lutheran Church in Milwaukee, WI.

Beginning music theory : a high school credit course / Bruce Benward, James E. Engel. Madison, Wis. : University Extension, University of Wisconsin, Independent Study, 1970. 2 v. : music ; 28 cm.

Let all the world in every corner sing / James Engel ; text by George Herbert (unpublished)

Notes: The following information was provided by Glenn Mahnke:

Two-part treble voices and keyboard.

It was written in performed in the early 1970s.

It was written for a music festival held at Northwest Lutheran School. The choir of Northwest was directed by Joel Mueller.

Mahnke recalls that the middle section of the piece was challenging vocally.

Messiah / G. F. Handel, arranged for male choir by James Engel (unpublished)

Notes: Arrangement for the male chorus of Concordia College, Milwaukee. Performed at Concordia College, Milwaukee.

Where e'er I go, what e'er my task / James Engel. Minneapolis, Minn. : Augsburg, 1978.

1 score (7 p.) ; 26 cm.

Notes: SATB a cappella – Condensed score provided for rehearsal purposes.

A manuscript copy was also found in the choral files at Gospel Evangelical Lutheran Church in Milwaukee, WI.

Works completed during James Engel's years at Dr. Martin Luther College in New Ulm, MN.

Christ, to Thee be glory [Manuscript] / Heinrich Schuetz ; edited, J. Engel. [n.d.]

1 score (8 p.) ; 24 cm.

Notes: SATB and rehearsal score

Manuscript found in the choral files at Martin Luther College in New Ulm, MN. The exact date is unknown but it was written during this time period.

Exsultate Deo [Manuscript] / Alessandro Scarlatti ; [edited by James Engel] [n.d.]

    1 score (8 p.)

    Notes: SATB

    James Engel is not listed on the score. The file copy index from Dr. Martin Luther College attributes this edition to him.

    Manuscript found in the choral files at Martin Luther College in New Ulm, MN. The exact date is unknown but it was written during this time period.

A manual for the beginning church organist / James Engel New Ulm, Minn. : James Engel, [n.d.]

    122 p. ; 28 cm.

    Notes: This manual has been used to teach organ students at Dr. Martin Luther College.

    The exact date is unknown, but it was written during this time period.

O FILII ET FILIAE [Manuscript] = O sons and daughters / Wolckmar Leisring; [edited by James Engel]

    1 score (8 p.)

    Notes: SSAATTBB

    James Engel is not listed on the score. The file copy index from Dr. Martin Luther College attributes this edition to him.

    Manuscript found in the choral files at Martin Luther College in New Ulm, MN. The exact date is unknown but it was written during this time period.

Ye need not toil nor languish [Manuscript] / Setting: James Engel. [n.d.]

    1 Score (1 p.)

    Notes: SATB

    Manuscript found in the choral files at Martin Luther College in New Ulm, MN. The exact date is unknown but it was written during this time period.

Zion, rise, Zion, rise / Arranged by James Engel; Original German text by Johann Schmidt; The translation is by Rev. Wm. Czamanske. Seattle, Wash : Aeolian Publ., [n.d.] 1 score (1 p.) ; 26 cm.

Notes: SATB a cappella.

Triumphant from the grave [Manuscript] / Text: W. Franzmann ; Tune: B. Backer ; Setting: J. Engel.

1975.

1 score (1 p.) ; 26 cm.

Notes: SATB

This choral piece is printed as a hymn in a number of Lutheran hymnals including Lutheran Worship and Christian Worship.

Manuscript found in the choral files at Martin Luther College in New Ulm, MN.

O depth of wealth [Manuscript] / James Engel. 1976.

1   score (8 p.) ; 26 cm.

Notes: SATB

Manuscript found in the choral files at Martin Luther College in New Ulm, MN.

God of the prophets / arr. James Engel. [Minneapolis, Minn.] : Augsburg, 1978. 1 score (4 p.) ; 26 cm.

Notes: SATB with rehearsal score.

I walk with angels / James Engel.

Springfield, Ohio : Chantry Music Press, 1978. 1 score (9 p.) ; 26 cm.

Note: SATB, 2 oboes, cello-bass and organ.

Chantry Press is now owned by Augsburg-Fortress.

[Copyrighted copy obtained by this author from Augsburg on June 15th, 2006]

Preludes on six hymntunes / James Engel. Minneapolis, Minn. : Augsburg, 1979. score (12 p.) ; 31 cm.

Contents:

How Sweet the Name of Jesus Sounds I Am Trusting You, Lord Jesus
Abide With Us, Our Savior Jesus, Refuge of the Weary
O Lord, How Shall I Meet You
To God the Holy Spirit Let Us Pray

Son of God, eternal Savior / arr. James Engel. [Minneapolis, Minn.] : Augsburg, 1979.

1 score (11 p.) ; 26 cm.

Notes: SATB and rehearsal score.

Three solos for medium voice / James Engel; Wilbur Held; Austin C Lovelace [Minneapolis, Minn.] : Augsburg, 1979.

2   scores (16 p. each) ; 31 cm. (Vocal Solo)

Contents:
Whither Thou Goest / James Engel.
Lord, Who at Cana's Wedding Feast / Wilbur Held.
O God of Love, Our Rest and Hope / Austin C. Lovelace.

As you go on your way / James Engel; Conrad Thompson. Minneapolis, Minn. : Augsburg, 1980.

1 score (4 p.) ; 27 cm.

Notes: (Vocal Solo)

"To Joan and Richard Mueller" (Joan Mueller is James Engel's daughter.)

Hymn preludes for Holy Communion : Volume III. St. Louis, Mo. : Concordia, 1980.

35 p. of music ; 28 cm.

Notes: Contains one work by James Engel.

Lord Jesus Christ, You Have Prepared / James Engel.

Eleven chorale preludes for organ / James Engel. New Ulm, Minn. : J. Engel, 1981.

1 score (25 p.) ; 28 cm.

Contents: Page:

From heaven above / arr. James Engel. [Minneapolis, Minn.] :
Augsburg, 1981. 1 score (12 p.) ; 26 cm.

Notes: SATB, 3 trumpets and optional congregation.

Dedicated to Richard Wegner.

A hymn of glory / arr. James Engel. [Minneapolis, Minn.] : Augsburg,
1981. 1 score (14 p.) ; 26 cm.

Notes: SATB, Junior Choir, Organ.

SSAA, ms. 41-49.

Hymn setting / Edward H. Meyer and James Engel. New Ulm, Minn.
: Dr. Martin Luther College, 1981. 1 score ; 28 cm.

Engel Music in this collection:
The King of Love My Shepherd Is
Once He Came in Blessing
Praise God the Lord, Ye Sons of Men*
Praise to the Lord, the Almighty
God Who Madest Earth and Heaven
Abide, O Dearest Jesus

Now Thank We All Our God
As with Gladness Men of Old

Notes: *(Prof. Engel and Dr. Meyer both contributed to this piece)

Jesus shall reign where'er the sun / arr. James Engel. Minneapolis, Minn. : Augsburg, 1982.

   1 score (12 p.) ; 26 cm.

   Notes: SATB with trumpet and optional congregation

Lift up your heads / Giovanni Gabrieli; James Engel. [Minneapolis, Minn.] : Augsburg, 1982.

   1 score (12 p.) ; 26 cm.

   Notes: For double chorus (SATB/SATB), and piano for rehearsal only./ Caption title.

   Giovanni Gabrieli ; [words from] Psalm 24:7-10 ; adapted, James Engel.

To us is born a little child : motet (SSATB) and carol (SATB) / James Engel; Valentin Neander. St. Louis, Mo. : Concordia, 1982.

   1 score (4 p.) ; 26 cm.

   Notes: Valentin Neander ; edited by James Engel.

Luther's liturgy / Martin Luther; James Engel. 1983 Anniversary ed. Milwaukee, WI : Northwestern, 1983. 19 p. ; 23 cm.

Music for the marriage service : with guidelines for planning the wedding. Kit 2. Minneapolis, Minn. : Augsburg, 1983.

   5 scores ; 26-31 cm. +; 1 booklet (4 p.) + 1 sound cassette (analog)

   Contents (Scores):
   As You Go on Your Way / James Engel And the Best Is Love / Richard Proulx
   Be Joyful in the Lord / Andre Campra ; ed. Robert J. Powell How Blest are They / Richard Proulx
   Three Solos for Medium Voice / by James Engel, Wilbur Held, Austin C. Lovelace
Organ preludes for the Passion season / James Engel. New Ulm, Minn. : J. Engel, 1983.

1 score (32, [1] p.) ; 29 cm.

Contents:

Three movements from the concerti grossi of Georg Friedrich Handel : arranged for organ / by James Engel; George Frideric Handel.

Springfield, Ohio : Chantry Music Press, 1983. 13 p. of music ; 30 cm.

Contents:
Concerto II. Allegro
Concerto III. Andante
Concerto IV. Larghetto.

Centennial organ collection.

New Ulm, Minn. : Dr. Martin Luther College, 1984. 1 score (39 p.) ; 30 cm.

Nineteen hymn introductions for the organ / James Engel. Milwaukee, Wis. : Northwestern, 1985.

33 p. of music ; 28 cm.

Contents:

Ten organ transcriptions from Opus 5 / Arcangelo Corelli. St. Louis, Mo. : Concordia, 1985

1 score (27 p.) ; 31 cm.

Notes: Preface by James Engel (p. 2)

Concordia hymn prelude series St. Louis, Mo. : Concordia, 1986. 42 v. + index.

DISTRESS	23	16
DOWN AMPNEY	12	28
HERZLICH LIEB	27	17, 22
HYMN TO JOY	27	36
KREMSER		42
MARTYDOM	31	40
NUN LASST UNS DEN LEIB BEGRABEN	34	16
O TRAURIGKEIT	8	32
RATHBUN	9	7
ST. GEORGES, WINDSOR	6	26
SCHÖNSTER HERR JESU	38	24
SUSSEX CARL	5	12
TRIMBUPH	11	30
VENI CREATOR SPIRITUS	13	12
WORCHESTER	13	38

An introduction to organ registration / James Engel. St. Louis, Mo. : Concordia, 1986.

44 p. : ill. ; 23 cm.

Sampler / Commission on Worship, Wisconsin Ev. Lutheran Synod. Milwaukee, Wis : Northwestern Pub. House, 1986.

1 score ; 23 cm.

Notes: Engel assisted Rev. K. Eggert behind the scenes and was not credited.

Hymn settings : Volume 2 / Edward H. Meyer and James Engel. New Ulm, Minn. : Dr. Martin Luther College, 1987.

1 score ; 28 cm.

Engel Music in this collection:
Lo, He Comes With Clouds Descending
Once in Royal David's City
Lamb of God, Pure and Holy
There Is a Green Hill Far Away
This Joyful Eastertide
Jesus Shall Reign Where'er the Sun
Amazing Grace

Abide with Me! Fast Falls the Eventide
What God Ordains is Always Good

God of the prophets / arr. James Engel. [Minneapolis, Minn.] : Augsburg, 1987. 1 score (12 p.) ; 26 cm.

Notes: SATB, organ, with optional congregation.

Christ is our cornerstone : Darwall's 148th / James Engel. St. Louis, Mo. : Concordia, 1988.

1 score (18 p.) + 1 chorus score (4 p.) + 5 parts ; 26 cm.

Notes: Anthem./ For chorus (SATB), children's choir (optional), congregation (optional), 3 trumpets, 2 trombones and organ./ Caption title./ Words printed as text inside back cover./ Pl. nos.: 98-2800 (score), 98-2823 (chorus score), 97-5981 (instrumental parts).

Dear Christians, one and all : a chorale concertato, for choir, congregation, trumpet and organ / Setting by James Engel.

St. Louis, Mo. : Concordia, 1988. 1 score (19 p.) ; 26 cm.

Notes: SAB choir.

Description above describes choral score. A full score can be purchased from CPH.

Lord of glory / arr. James Engel. Minneapolis, Minn. : Augsburg, 1988. 1 score (8 p.) ; 26 cm.

Notes: SATB with flute.

Twenty hymn introduction for the organ / James Engel. Milwaukee, Wis. : Northwestern, 1988.

1 score (32 p.) ; 28 cm.

Contents:	Page:
ACH BLEIB BEI UNS	20
ACH, WAS SOL ICH SUENDER MACHEN	15
BOYLSTON	26
DIADEMATA	9
DUNDEE	30
ERHALT UNS, HERR	13

James Engel's Posthumous Works.

Remember, Lord, the times you called me / Text: Jaroslav J. Vajda ; Setting: James Engel. St. Louis, Mo. : Morning Star, 1989.

> 1 score (10 p.) ; 26 cm.

> Notes: SATB, organ, and opt. Congregation.

See there, the Lord comes / Dietrich Buxtehude ; edited by James Engel. St. Louis, Mo. : Morning Star, 1989.

> 1 score (10 p.) ; 26 cm.

Variations on In dulci jubilo / James Engel St. Louis, Mo. : Concordia, 1989

> 17 p. of music ; 31 cm.

A little chaconne on a Lenten hymn : O MEIN JESU, ICH MUSS STERBEN : geistliche Volkslieder, Paderborn, 1850 / James Engel.

> St. Louis, Mo. : Morning Star, 1990. 6 p. of music ; 31 cm.

My song is love unknown : concertato for choir (SATB), congregation, instrument in C, and organ / [tune], LOVE UNKNOWN [by] John Ireland ; setting by James Engel ; [text], Samuel Crossman.

St. Louis, Mo. : Morning Star, 1990. 1 score and part (11 p.) ; 26 cm.

Notes: Congregation part printed on p. 2 of score; instrumentalist plays from main score.

Pastorale on Jesus Christ, my sure defense = JESUS, MEINE ZUVERSICHT: two flutes and keyboard / James Engel.

St. Louis, Mo. : Morning Star, 1990.

1 score (3 p.) ; 31 cm.; + 2 parts ([1] p. each) ; 28 cm.

Note: based on the tune by Johann Crüger; setting by James Engel.

Pour down, O Holy Spirit / James Engel. St. Louis, Mo. : Morning Star, 1991.

4 p. ; 26 cm.

Notes: SATB and opt. keyboard.

Two Christmas plainsongs for male chorus / James Engel. St. Louis, Mo. : Morning Star, 1991.

1 score (7 p.) ; 26 cm.

1. Oh, Come, Oh, Come, Emmanuel (VENI EMMANUEL) TTBB and Keyboard.
2. Of the Father's Love Begotten (DIVINUM MYSTERIUM) Unison voices and organ.

9 easy chorale preludes for the Christmas season / James Engel. St. Louis, Mo. : Morning Star, 1993.

1 score (20 p.) ; 28 cm.

Contents:	Page:
ES IS EIN ROS	10
IN DULCI JUBILO	12
LASST UNS ALLE	18
NUN KOMM, DER HEIDEN HEILAND	8
O JESU CHRIST, DEIN KRIPPLEIN	16
PUER NOBIS	6
VENI EMMANUEL	4

| VOM HIMMEL HOCH | 20 |
| W ZLOBIE LEZY | 14 |

Notes: Republished from: Eleven chorale preludes for organ / James Engel.

Two works were not republished in this new set: Lord, to Thee I Make Confession – Settings one and two. [HERR, ICH HABE MISSGEHANDELT]

9 easy chorale preludes for Lent / James Engel. St. Louis, Mo. : Morning Star, 1994.

1 score (27 p.) ; 25 cm.

Contents:	Page:
CHRISTE, DU LAMM GOTTES - I	10
CHRISTE, DU LAMM GOTTES - II	12
CHRISTE, DU LAMM GOTTES - III	14
DER AM KREUZ	8
HERZLIEBSTER JESU	4
JESU KREUZ, LEIDEN UND PEIN	2
O TRAURIGKEIT	24
SOUTHWELL	17
VALET WILL ICH DIR GEBEN - 11	18
VATER UNSER	26
WINCHESTER NEW	22

Notes: Republished from: Organ preludes for the Passion season / James Engel. One work is not republished in this set: The Royal Banners Forward Go. [VEXILLA REGIS]

For years on years of matchless grace : SATB and organ / James Engel ; [text by] Werner H. Franzmann.

St. Louis, Mo. : Morning Star, 1994. 1 score (7 p.) ; 26 cm.

Note: Tune name is FOX VALLEY

Genre

Organ

9 easy chorale preludes for the Christmas season / James Engel.
9 easy chorale preludes for Lent / James Engel.

Centennial organ collection. Concordia hymn prelude series

DISTRESS	23	16
DOWN AMPNEY	12	28
HERZLICH LIEB	27	17, 22
HYMN TO JOY	27	36
KREMSER	29	42
MARTYRDOM	31	40
NUN LASS UNS DEN LEIB BEGRABEN	34	16
O TRAURIGKEIT	8	32
RATHBUN	9	7
ST. GEORGE'S, WINDSOR	6	26
SCHÖNSTER HERR JESU	38	24
SUSSEX CAROL	5	12
TRIUMPH	11	30
VENI CREATOR SPIRITUS	13	12
WORCESTER	13	38

Eleven chorale preludes : for organ / James Engel.

Hymn preludes for Holy Communion : Volume III.
Contains: Lord Jesus Christ, you have prepared / James Engel.

Let all the World in every corner sing / James Engel ; text by George Herbert (unpublished)

A little chaconne on a Lenten hymn : O MEIN JESU, ICH MUSS STERBEN : geistliche Volkslieder, Paderborn, 1850 / James Engel.

Nineteen hymn introductions for the organ / James Engel. Organ preludes for the Passion season / James Engel.

Preludes on six hymntunes / James Engel.

Three movements from the concerti grossi of Georg Friedrich Handel : arranged for organ / by James Engel; George Frideric Handel.

Twenty hymn introduction for the organ / James Engel. Two chorale preludes / James Engel

Variations on IN DULCI JUBILO / James Engel

Instrumental

Pastorale on Jesus Christ, my sure defense = JESUS, MEINE ZUVERSICHT : two flutes and keyboard / James Engel

Vocal

A hymn of glory / arr. James Engel.

As you go on your way / James Engel; Conrad Thompson. Christ is our cornerstone : DARWALL'S 148TH / James Engel.

Dear Christians, one and all : a chorale concertato, for choir, congregation, trumpet and organ / Setting by James Engel.

For years on years of matchless grace : SATB and organ / James Engel ; [text by] Werner H. Franzmann.

From heaven above / arr. James Engel.

God of the prophets / arr. James Engel. (1978) God of the prophets / arr. James Engel. (1987)

Hymn settings / Edward H. Meyer and James Engel.
Engel music in this collection:
The King of Love My Shepherd Is
Once He Came in Blessing
Praise God the Lord, Ye Sons of Men*
Praise to the Lord, the Almighty
God, Who Madest the Earth and Heaven
Abide, O Dearest Jesus
Now Thank We All Our God
As With Gladness Men of Old
Notes: *(Prof. Engel and Dr. Meyer both contributed to this piece)

Hymn settings : Volume 2 / Edward H. Meyer and James Engel.
Engel Music in this collection:
Lo, He Comes with Clouds Descending
Once in Royal David's City
Lamb of God, Pure and Holy
There Is a Green Hill Far Away
This Joyful Eastertide
Jesus Shall Reign Where'er the Sun
Amazing Grace
Abide with Me! Fast Falls the Eventide
What God Ordains Is Always Good

I walk with angels / James Engel.

Jesus shall reign where'er the sun / arr. James Engel.

Music for the marriage service : with guidelines for planning the wedding. Kit 2. Engel music in this volume: As You Go on Your Way / James Engel

Three Solos for Medium Voice / by James Engel, Wilbur Held, Austin C. Lovelace

My song is love unknown : concertato for choir (SATB), congregation, instrument in C, and organ / [tune], LOVE UNKNOWN [by] John Ireland ; setting by James Engel ; [text], Samuel Crossman.

Lord of glory / arr. James Engel.

O depth of wealth [Manuscript] / James Engel. Pour down, O Holy Spirit / James Engel.

Remember, Lord, the times you called me / Text: Jaroslav J. Vajda ; Setting: James Engel. Silent night [Manuscript] : verse two / James Engel.

Son of God, eternal Savior / arr. James Engel.

Three solos for medium voice / James Engel; Wilbur Held; Austin C Lovelace Engel music in this volume: Whither Thou Goest / James Engel.

Triumphant from the grave [Manuscript] / Text: W. Franzmann ; Tune: B. Backer ; Setting: J. Engel.

Two Christmas plainsongs for male chorus / James Engel. Where e'er I go, what e'er my task / James Engel.

Ye need not toil nor languish [Manuscript] / Setting: James Engel.

Zion, rise, Zion, rise / Arranged by James Engel; Original German text by Johann Schmidt;

Hymnal & Liturgical Material

Luther's liturgy / Martin Luther; James Engel

Sampler / Commission on Worship, Wisconsin Ev. Lutheran Synod.

Works by other composers edited by James Engel

Christ, to thee be glory [Manuscript] / Heinrich Schuetz ; edited, J. Engel. Exsultate Deo [Manuscript] / Alessandro Scarlatti ; [edited by James Engel] Lift up your heads / Giovanni Gabrieli; James Engel.

Messiah / G. F. Handel, arranged for male choir by James Engel (unpublished)

O FILII ET FILIAE [Manuscript] = O sons and daughters / Wolckmar Leisring; [edited by James Engel]

Ten organ transcriptions from Opus 5 / Arcangelo Corelli.
    Notes: Preface by James Engel (p. 2)

To us is born a little child : motet (SSATB) and carol (SATB) / James Engel; Valentin Neander. See there, the Lord comes / Dietrich Buxtehude ; edited by James Engel.

Organ Methods Courses:

A manual for the beginning church organist / James Engel

Beginning music theory : a high school credit course / Bruce Benward, James E. Engel. An introduction to organ registration / James Engel.

Pictures of James Engel, His Family and Friends

Engel family picture.

Back Row: Carl, John, Dorothy, and Lucille.
Front Row: Father (Carl), James, Paul, Janet, Mother (Emma), and Ruth.

From: Janet Engel

James Engel and Paul Manz in the summer of 1947.

From: Dr. Richard Wegner.

Lutheran A Cappella Choir

Undated picture – taken at Immanuel Lutheran Church, Milwaukee.

Lutheran A Cappella Choir – Close-up.
(James Engel is at the right end of the upper row.)

Undated picture – taken at Immanuel Lutheran Church, Milwaukee.

Prof. James Engel and Mr. Grant Malme at their pianos.

Malme and Engel at the piano

From: "Masters give duo-piano recital." *Concordia Courier* 28, no. 2 [March 21, 1960]: 3.

Henry Wegner and James Engel

From: Dr. Richard Wegner

Appendix | 127

Concordia Chapel
to Get New Organ

Against a background of the Wartburg mural in the Luther Room, Mr. Werner Bosch (left), of Kassel, Germany, joins Prof. James E. Engel, Chairman of Concordia's Department of Music, in a study of plans for the new chapel organ of Concordia College to be installed during the summer of 1963.

From: *Concordia Courier*, September 28, 1962, Page 4.

LISTENING TO THE vibrant tones of the Concordia chapel organ is sweet music to the ears of President Walter W. Stuenkel (left) and Music Director James Engel, especially since Concordia has received a refund on the organ's costs.

From: *Concordia Courier*, May 21, 1965, p. 5

James Engel at the console

From: *Concordia Blue and White*, 1971 (Faculty Picture)

James Engel Directing the DMLC College Choir – 1979

James Engel at the DMLC Choir Room organ

From: Excelsior (Top picture, 1979 and Bottom picture, 1989)

Dorothy Croll, Dr. Richard Wegner and Mary Geis

Taken at Immanuel Lutheran Church, Baltimore, MD on May 22, 2008.

Churches and Schools of Engel's Life and Career

Bethlehem Lutheran School (1930s)

From: Bethlehem Lutheran School: Page 11.

Bethlehem Lutheran Church

St John Lutheran Church – Exterior

Interior of the sanctuary from the time Engel served St. John Lutheran Church

Bottom picture from: St. John Lutheran Church Anniversary Booklet.

Appendix | 135

Gospel Evangelical Lutheran Church in Milwaukee, Wisconsin.

Fox Valley Lutheran High School

St. Peter Lutheran Church

St. John Lutheran Church in Sleepy Eye, Minnesota.

Pipe Organs at Institutions Engel Served

Schulke organ as James Engel knew it
Picture from: Bethlehem Lutheran Church – Anniversary Booklet

The Schulke organ today

Current Stop List of the Schulke Organ at Bethlehem Lutheran Church

Great:		Swell:		Pedal	
8′	Principal	16′	Bourdon	32′	Untersatz (Resultant from 16′ Lieblich)
8′	Hohlflöte (Missing at time of visit)	8′	Geigen Principal	16′	Subbass
8′	Gedeckt	8′	Lieblich Gedeckt	16′	Lieblich Gedeckt
8′	Gemshorn	8′	Salicional	8′	Octave Bass
4′	Octave	8′	Voix Celeste	8′	Gedeckt Bass
4′	Nachthorn	4′	Traverse Flöte	4′	Octave
2 2/3′	Quinte	4′	Flute D'amour	16′	Fagott
2′	Super Octave	2 2/3′	Nasat	8′	Great to Pedal
III	Mixture	2′	Waldflöte	8′	Swell to Pedal
8′	Trumpet	1 3/5′	Terz	4′	Swell to Pedal
4′	Great to Great Coupler	III	Mixture (from Great)		
8′	Swell to Great Coupler	8′	Oboe		
		8′	Clarinet		
		16′	Swell to Swell		
			Swell Unison Off		
		4′	Swell to Swell		

The organ, in its present disposition, was renovated in 1997. Approximately 276 pipes were added to the organ at that time, along with a different (used) console and solid-state switching. Currently the organ is reported to have 1,290 pipes. Mr. Richard Weber, Bethlehem's organist, was in charge of the most recent renovation and additions.1 The organ's pipework is housed in a beautiful case, which was constructed in the typical Schulke style. The whole instrument, with the exception of the lowest 12 pipes of the 16′ Lieblich Gedeckt, is under common expression. Those 12 pipes are located on the left side of the case. The present organ façade consists of non-speaking pipework. The pictures above and on page 139 illustrate the difference between the older pipe screen configuration and the current dummy façade pipes. (From Richard Weber, *Bethlehem's Pipe Organ*.)

The Kilgen Organ as James Engel knew it.

St. John Lutheran Church Anniversary Booklet

The Schlicker Organ in 2007

Schlicker Organ at St. John's Lutheran in Racine

Great	Swell	Positiv	Pedal
16' Pommer	8' Gedeckt (from Kilgen)	8' Quintadena	32' Untersatz
8' Principal	8' Salicional	4' Principal	16' Principal (from Kilgen)
8' Rohr Floete	8' Celeste	4' Rohr Floete	16' Subbass (from Kilgen)
4' Octave	4' Principal	2'2/3' Nasat	16' Pommer
4' Spitz Floete	4' Hohl Floete	2' Octave	8' Principal (from Kilgen)
2' Hohl Floete	2' Block Floete	1 3/5' Terz	8' Gedeckt
1 1/3' Larigot	1' Siffloete	IV Zimbel	4' Choral Bass
IV Mixture	IV Scharf	16' Dulzian	II Rauschpfeife
8' Trumpet	16' Dulzian	8' Krummhorn	IV Mixture
Chimes	8' Oboe Schalmei	8' Festlich Trompete	32' Kontra Posaune
16' Swell to Great	4' Clarion	Zimbelstern	16' Posaune
8' Swell to Great	Tremolo	Tremolo	16' Dulzian
4' Swell to Great	16' Swell to Swell	16' Swell to Positiv	8' Trumpet
16' Positiv to Great	Swell Off	8' Swell to Positiv	4' Cornet (from Kilgen)
8' Positiv to Great	4' Swell to Swell	4' Swell to Positiv	Chimes
MIDI on Great	16' Positiv to Swell	MIDI on Positiv	8' Great to Pedal
	MIDI on Swell		4' Great to Pedal
			8' Swell to Pedal
			4' Swell to Pedal
			8' Positiv to Pedal
			MIDI on Pedal

Further additions to the Schlicker organ and incorporation of the old Kilgen organ.

Over the years the Schlicker organ has grown into a impressive 52-rank instrument. The organ comes complete with Festival Trumpets and two electronic 32' stops. The console is also prepared for the addition of a MIDI interface when funds someday become available to add it. The MIDI interface connection, when installed, will allow a person to hook up a digital instrument directly to the organ. This interface allows external digital sound devices to be accessible to the organist or allow the pipes of the organ to be controlled remotely from another MIDI equipped instrument (piano, keyboard, guitar, etc.).

Five ranks of the old Kilgen organ survive in the present instrument, but they were repaired and revoiced by the Schlicker company. The 8' Gedeckt on the Swell was from the Kilgen, and the other four ranks can be found in the pedal organ. These pedal ranks are the 16' Principal, the 16' Subbass, the 8' Principal, and the 4' Cornet.[2] The 4' Cornet on this instrument is a reed stop and should not be confused with the typical Cornet stop composed of mutation ranks. It was originally the Oboe in the Kilgen instrument. This stop's current voicing is distinctly brighter than that of typical Oboe stops. The façade of the Kilgen organ was retained and updated with Festival Trumpet pipes and a Zimbelstern. (From Arthur Preuss, Interview by author, Racine, WI, June 15, 2007.)

Appendix | 143

Concordia Chapel Organ at Dedication

From: Concordia Courier, Nov. 30, 1963, Page 1.

Resources of the Werner Bosch Organ, Opus 333:

Hauptwerk:		
Prinzipal	8'	56 pipes
Gedackt	8'	56 pipes
Prinzipal	4'	56 pipes
Rohrflöte	4'	56 pipes
Flachflöte	2'	56 pipes
Klein Nasatl	1/3'	56 pipes
Mixture V	1'	280 pipes
Krummhorn Tremolant		
Schwellwerk to Hauptwerk		

Schwellwerk:		
Holzgedackt	8'	56 pipes
Spitzgambe	8'	56 pipes
Schwebung (t.c.)	8'	44 pipes
Koppelflöte	4'	56 pipes
Nasat	2 2/3'	56 pipes
Prinzipal	2'	56 pipes
Blockflöte	2'	56 pipes
Terz		
Scharf IV		
Rankett		
(l/4 mahogany resonators)		
Schalmei-Oboe	8'	56 pipes
Tremolant		

Pedal:		
Subbass	16'	32 pipes
Prinzipal	8'	32 pipes
Spitzgedackt	8'	32 pipes
Choralbass	4'	32 pipes
Nachthorn	2'	32 pipes
Fagott	16'	32 pipes
Rohr Schalmei	4'	32 pipes
Hauptwerk to Pedal		
Schwellwerk to Pedal		
Zimbelstern		

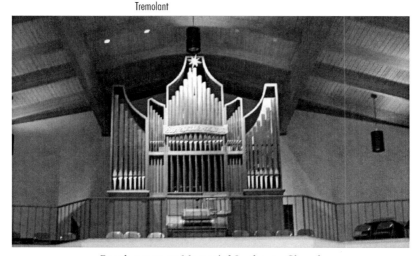

Bosch organ at Memorial Lutheran Church

Specification changes to the organ since its installation at Memorial Lutheran.

Since the dedication, Memorial Lutheran has made a number of changes to the instrument. The congregation employed the Martin Ott Organ Company of St. Louis, Missouri to accomplish this. The Ott Organ Company is known for its work with mechanical action pipe organs and German-American pipe voicing. The roll-top, which allowed the console key-desk to be closed, was removed so that the console is now permanently open. The Martin Ott Organ Company replaced the old music rack with one that includes their distinctive wooden inlay design. They replaced the stop rail (where the stops controls are located), added solid state memory (to control the stop changing pistons) and added toe studs (stop changing pistons for the feet) in order to make the organ more versatile. Two electronic 32' stops were added — of the flue variety. The Great Krummhorn was replaced with a vibrant trumpet stop. There is a stop-tab provided on the console that is reserved for the Krummhorn. The congregation could add this rank back into the organ specification. However, they would need to provide a separate electric action chest and winding outside of the current organ case in order to bring it back into service. The Swell 2' Principal was shifted to bring it down to a 4' Principal, and the IV-rank Scharff was modified.3 This instrument, in its current condition, is an exciting and beautiful instrument to play.. (From James Burmeister, Interview by author, Glendale, WI, April 25, 2007)

Appendix | 145

The Bosch organ console in 2007

Inside the Bosch organ

Organ at Gospel Lutheran Church

Gospel Organ Specifications

Great:	Swell:	Pedal:
8′ Principal	8′ Rohr Floete	16′ Bourdon
8′ Holz Gedeckt	8′ Salicional	8′ Principal
4′ Principal	8 Voix Celeste	8′ Bourdon
4′ Koppel Floete	4′ Flute	4′ Choral Bass
2 2/3′ Rohr Nazard	2′ Principal	4′ Flute
2′ Block Floete	II Sesquialtera	2′ Block Floete
IV Mixture	8′ Fagot	16′ Fagot
8′ Fagot	4′ Fagot	8′ Fagot
4′ Great to Great	16′ Swell to Swell	4′ Fagot
16′ Swell to Great	4′ Swell to Swell	8′ Great to Pedal
8′ Swell to Great	Swell Unison Off	8′ Swell to Pedal
4′ Swell to Great		4′ Swell to Pedal
Chimes	Zimbelstern (by Gary Foxe)	

Further information about the organ

The newly rebuilt organ suffered some damage during the fire and needed repair. This was undertaken after Engel had moved to Appleton. In 1974, when Peters was asked to service the instrument, he found that "both the windchests and even new pipework were covered with the residue" from the fire of December 1971. "The exposed leather on reservoirs was damaged from the effects of heat, smoke and humidity, as well as pipework and mechanicals, but showed no sign of direct fire damage." Significant damage to the organ needed to be repaired, but the work was undertaken two years after Engel had moved to Appleton. Peters also commented that Otto Eberle, the man who had rebuilt the Gospel Organ in 1968, was in poor health and had not been able to complete certain work on the organ. Since Eberle died in 1974, the Peters and Weiland Organ Company was called in to finish the work. "We were asked to install the bass of the 8′ Rohr Flute and 4′ Swell flute as well as some minor repairs, which we did in the summer of 1974. The instrument still needed additional work such as cleaning of the pipework, re-leathering of the reservoirs and a new windchest for the 16-8′ Fagott, 2′ Principal and II Sesquialtera that we undertook in 1979."4. (From Stanton Peters, December 31, 2007, letter to author.)

Bulletin from the Organ Dedication
at Gospel Lutheran Church

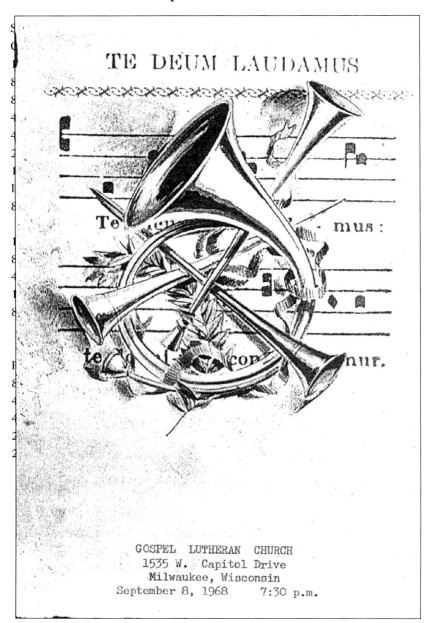

The church organ which we dedicate this day serves in a number of differing capacities. In addition to accompanying the congregation in its hymns and liturgy, it is used to accompany choir anthems, solo instruments and voices, and frequently as a solo instrument itself within the worship service. In this latter function it has much to say to the worshipper. As such it can reflect and reinforce the various attitudes and phases of Christian life.

Such is the purpose of the organ program this day of dedication, briefly considering the Christian attitudes of trust, prayer, praise, and hope.

Chorales from the church steeple   Brass ensemble

Processional   Martin Shaw

Hymn #39

     Stanza 1:   Choir
     Stanzas 2 and 3:   Congregation
     Stanza 4:   Choir
     Stanza 5:   Congregation

The Vesper Liturgy

     V: O Lord, open Thou my lips.
     R: And my mouth shall show forth Thy praise.
     V: Make haste, O God, to deliver me.
     R: Make haste to help me, O Lord,
          Gloria Patri

The Psalmody

Choir: O Clap Your Hands   Harald Rohlig

The Organ

     A Mighty Fortress is Our God   Walter Schindler

        An energetic contemporary setting in the
        form of a fantasy by a young German com-
        poser.

Sonata III   Felix Mendelssohn

    Mendelssohn, a Jew converted to the Lutheran
faith, wrote six organ sonatas.   Luther's
sturdy chorale of penitence,   "Out of the
Depths Have I Cried Unto Thee,"   serves as
the pedal theme of the central part of this
sonata over which Mendelssohn constructed an
intense fugue.

All Praise To God Who Reigns Above   Helmut Walcha

    Although blind, this contemporary German com-
poser has gained world recognition for his excellent settings of many Lutheran chorales as
well as his excellent recordings of the works
of J. S. Bach.

Wake Awake, for Night is Flying   Flor Peeters

    Flor Peeters is the outstanding Dutch compo-
ser of our day.   The rapid manual passages
played on the flute ranks reflect the joy of
the five wise virgins prepared for the coming of the Lord. The more sombre reed melody
represents the ominous warning of this chorale (L.H. 609).

My Heart is Filled With Longing   Johannes Brahms

    The tune is more frequently associated with
the words of the great Passion Chorale, "Oh
Sacred Head", and brings to the listener's
mind the reason for the peacefulness of our
departure. The text used by Brahms:

            My heart is filled with longing
                To pass away in peace,
          For woes are round me thronging,
                And trials will not cease.
         O fain would I be hasting
                From thee, dark world of gloom,
         To gladness everlasting;
                Oh Jesus, quickly come!

Mein Junges Leben Hat Ein End   Jan Pieter Sweelinck

To the Dutch composer, Sweelinck, belongs much
of the credit for the high level of keyboard
music of the 17th century. The downward step-
wise progressions of the early phrases of the
tune reflect peaceful resignation. A delight-
ful set of variations on the tune follows.

Hymn #123   Congregation and Choir

Dr. Paul Manz, Concordia College, St. Paul,
Minn., has graciously consented to let us
use his unpublished manuscript of interludes during this hymn. The interludes will
precede stanzas 3, 4, 6, 7, 8.

This was before
it was published-
I had a hand-
written copy

The offerings will be gathered

The dedication of the organ

Choir: How Beautiful are the Messengers

                                        Felix Mendelssohn
Collect for the Ministry

Choir: How Beautiful are Thy Dwellings   Johannes Brahms

Collect for the Church

Benediction

Rev. Ed. A. Krause, Pastor

Gospel Lutheran Church Choir

Concordia College Brass Ensemble
Duane Davis, Harold Hintzmann
Robert Schaefer, Robert Bartel

James Engel, Organist

Art by Alice Housner

CPH LITHO IN U. S. A. 84-2408

Weickhardt Organ at St. Peter Ev. Lutheran Church

(This organ was decommissioned after a new sanctuary was built in 2014. The organ was removed and the pipes were recycled into another instrument by the Richard Swanson Organ Company of Grand Ledge, MI.)

The original stop list was as follows:

8′	Open Diapason	Chimes (with mini keyboard)
8′	Melodia	Sub Octave Coupler
8′	Gamba	Super Octave Coupler
4′	Octave	Manual to Pedal
4′	Flute Harmonique	Tremolo
16′	Pedal Bourdon	

Organ at St. John Lutheran Church, Sleepy Eye, Minnesota

APPENDIX D

Other Documents

DR. MARTIN LUTHER COLLEGE

NEW ULM, MINNESOTA 56073
TELEPHONE 507 / 354-8221

College Choir

December 28, 1982

Dear Dick and Vi,

After months of absolutely beautiful snowless weather, last evening it started coming down and once more we are well aware we are in the middle of Minnesota. Snow drifts piled up this morning higher than my snow blower. Luckily my son and son-in-law were still visiting with their families - so I had plenty of help with this blizzard. We went through a most pleasant Christmas with children and grandchildren back home with us for a few days. Together we had opportunity to worship at St. John's church in Sleepy Eye with the children's service. Norma still teaches out there, and starting this year and for at least one more I am full time organist.

Your '81 Christmas card and programs came through the mail very well. They were on my desk in my office for a full year, waiting patiently to be answered. I am very sorry about that. I promise to be much more prompt answering your letters.

Dick, your Faure arrangement is excellent! I hope CPH will advertise it not only in the Unison section, but also in their wedding solo selections. It seems to fit very well for weddings. I certainly will use it and will do some encouraging in our circles. You must do more!

I truly appreciate your willingness to do the anthems I've sent, especially the "From Heaven Above". Many copies now have been sold, . . more this Christmas than last. Augsburg now has three more anthems in the process. I will send them when they get off the press.

I have eight organ seminars to conduct throughout Minnesota and Wisconsin during our Spring break which comes toward the end of February. I will have of your Blessed Jesus along with me and intend to go through it with them.

Also herewith I include Eleven Chorale Preludes. These were written about a year ago at the request of our Music Department chairman to fill a gap in our organ teaching program. The problem is that we admit students on the organ too early, with only a minimum of piano. The piano department is much too lenient about sending them on to us. I has been a struggle finding both a method book and easy compositions for them to play in their first months. These Eleven were constructed to give these beginners opportunity to get the feel of the whole organ - pedals, and both manuals. Usually the kids who begin in September can master them all by Christmas and they love to assist at the organ at Christmas time. Hugo uses them and a number of other colleges have now begun to use them . A second set of Lenten preludes is already to be typed. The typing is done on our new Olympia music typewriter.

$\left(\text{over} \right)$

Letter from James Engel to Richard Wegner

Had several pleasant visits with Hugo this past summer. I had a
week of Organ Seminar with 13 students in the Milwaukee area - this
gave me chance to visit old friends. Hugo and Selda are doing
very well. Concordia Milwaukee has purchased a new college site
on Lake Michigan - a beautiful area! They are going to move the
organ to the new chapel - it should sound great!

I hope this finds you both well - Norma and I wish you both and
your family a blessed New Year.

Jim

From: Dr. Richard Wegner

Engel Funeral Bulletin

THE CHRISTIAN FUNERAL SERVICE
FOR
JAMES EDWARD ENGEL
THURSDAY, APRIL 20, 1989   1:30 o'clock

PRESERVICE ANTHEM   D M L C Treble Choir
   "I Walk With Angels All The Way"   J. Engel

   I.   Sinfonia

   II.   Recitative
         In dark of night, or yet in days beset with strife,
         Thy gracious loving hand, O Lord, sustains;
         For Thou dost give thine angels charge,
         Who in their silent, tireless care
         Surround with their protecting arm
         Thy children frail who wander paths unknown.

   III. Aria
         I walk with angels all the way
         They shield me and befriend me;
         All satan's pow'r is held at bay
         When heav'nly hosts attend me.
         They are a sure defense.
         All fears and sorrows hence,
         Unharmed by foes, do what they may,
         I walk with angels all the way.

   IV.   Chorale
         My walk is heav'nward all the way;
         Await, my soul, the morrow,
         When thou shalt find release for aye
         From all thy sin and sorrow.
         With Christ, my Savior, Guide,
         And angel hosts beside
         For all the world, I would not stay;
         My walk is heav'nward all the way!

   Accompanists: Cindy Techlin, flute
                  Grace Wessel, flute
                  Beth Sievert, organ
                  Grace Bartel, cello

IN THE NAME OF
THE FATHER AND OF THE SON AND OF THE HOLY SPIRIT. AMEN.

THE OBITUARY [Read by the Pastor]

THE ANTHEM
"Lord, Let At Last Thine Angels Come"

D M L C College Choir
Hans Leo Hassler

Lord, let at last thine angels come
To Abram's bosom bear me home,
That I may die unfearing;
Then in its narrow chamber keep
My body safe in painless sleep
Until thy reappearing;

And then from death awaken me,
That these mine eyes with joy may see,
O Son of God, thy glorious face,
My Savior and my Fount of Grace!

Lord Jesus Christ, my prayer attend,
And I will praise thee without end.

THE EXHORTATION AND THE PSALM 23

THE SCRIPTURE LESSON   II Corinthians 4

THE HYMN 195   "Christ Jesus Lay In Death's Strong Bands"
The congregation is asked to join in singing the hymns.

1. Christ Jesus lay in death's strong bands,
   For our offenses given;
   But now at God's right hand He stands
   And brings us life from heaven;
   Therefore let us joyful be
   And sing to God right thankfully
   Loud songs of hallelujah.
   Hallelujah!

2. It was a strange and dreadful strife
   When Life and Death contended;
   The victory remained with Life,
   The reign of Death was ended;
   Holy Scripture plainly saith
   That Death is swallowed up by Death,
   His sting is lost forever.
   Hallelujah!

3. Here the true Paschal Lamb we see,
   Whom God so freely gave us;
   He died on the accursed tree
   So strong His love! to save us.
   See, His blood doth mark our door;
   Faith points to it, Death passes o'er,
   And Satan cannot harm us.
   Hallelujah!

4. So let us keep the festival
   Whereto the Lord invites us;
   Christ is Himself the Joy of all,
   The Sun that warms and lights us.
   By His grace He doth impart
   Eternal sunshine to the heart;
   The night of sin is ended.
   Hallelujah!

5. Then let us feast this Easter Day
   On Christ, the Bread of heaven;
   The Word of Grace hath purged away
   The old and evil leaven.
   Christ alone our souls will feed,
   He is our meat and drink indeed;
   Faith lives upon no other. Hallelujah!

THE SERMON   I Corinthians 15:54-58
      "DEATH HAS BEEN SWALLOWED UP IN VICTORY.
      THANKS BE TO GOD! HE GIVES US THE VICTORY
            THROUGH OUR LORD JESUS CHRIST."

THE HYMN 707   "This Joyful Easter Tide"

1. This joyful Eastertide,
   Away with sin and sorrow!
   My love, the Crucified,
   Has sprung to life this morrow:
   Had Christ, who once was slain,
   Not burst his three-day prison,
   Our faith had been in vain.
   But now has Christ arisen, arisen, arisen;
   But now has Christ arisen!

2. Death's flood has lost its chill
   Since Jesus crossed the river;
   Lover of souls, from ill
   My passing soul deliver:
   Had Christ, who once was slain,
   Not burst his three-day prison,
   Our faith had been in vain.
   But now has Christ arisen, arisen, arisen;
   But now has Christ arisen!

Appendix | 159

3. My flesh in hope shall rest
And for a season slumber
Till trump from east to west
Shall wake the dead in number:
Had Christ, who once was slain,
Not burst his three-day prison,
Our faith had been in vain.
But now has Christ arisen, arisen, arisen;
But now has Christ arisen!

THE PRAYER

THE LORD'S PRAYER

THE BENEDICTION
The Lord bless you and keep you.
The Lord make His face shine upon you and be gracious unto you.
The Lord look upon you with favor and give you peace. Amen.

THE OFFICIANTS:	Rev. James D. Liggett Jr.
	Professor Arnold Koelpin
THE ORGANIST:	Professor Francis Schubkegel
THE CHOIRS:	DMLC Treble Choir
	Joyce C. Schubkegel, Director
	DMLC College Choir
	Roger A. Hermanson, Director
THE PALLBEARERS:	Professor Ames Anderson
	Professor Bruce Backer
	Professor Fred Bartel
	Professor Charles Luedtke
	Professor Edward Meyer
	Professor John Nolte
	Professor Otto Schenk
	Professor Ronald Shilling
	Professor Wayne Wagner

JAMES EDWARD ENGEL

Child of God and brother in Christ.

He was born March 21, 1925 in Milwaukee, Wisconsin to Carl Engel and Emma nee Eggert.

He was received into the Kingdom of God by the washing of Infant Baptism on April 12, 1925 at Jerusalem Evangelical Lutheran Church in Milwaukee by Pastor H. Gieschen.

He reaffirmed his baptismal covenant with God in his Confirmation on April 10, 1938 at Bethlehem Ev. Lutheran Church in Milwaukee by Pastor Oscar Kaiser.

He was united by God in Holy Matrimony with Norma nee Hasz on July 12, 1947 at St. Paul's Ev. Lutheran Church in Mt. Prospect, Illinois by Pastor J.E.A. Mueller.

He served the Wisconsin Evangelical Lutheran Synod at Dr. Martin Luther College in New Ulm and Fox Valley Lutheran High School in Appleton, Wisconsin. He served the Lutheran Church-Missouri Synod at Bethlehem Lutheran Church in Milwaukee, St. John's Lutheran Church in Racine, Wisconsin and Concordia College in Milwaukee.

He was a member of St. John's Evangelical Lutheran Church of Sleepy Eye.

He was translated into the eternal kingdom of Glory on Monday, April 17th having attained the age of 64 years and 27 days.

He is survived by his wife: Norma; his son: James Jr.; his daughters: Kathleen (Gary) Kennedy, Mary Poetter, Joan (Richard) Mueller; his brothers: Carl, John and Paul; his sisters: Dorothy Schmelin., Lucille Mueller, Ruth Kent, Janet Engel; 8 grandchildren; other relatives and friends; St. John's Congregation and the entire Christian Church on earth. We sorrow at his departure from us but rejoice at his entrance into heaven, where all believers in Christ will be finally reunited forever in the presence of God.

* * * * * * * * * *

A light lunch will be served immediately after this service on the campus of Dr. Martin Luther College. Everyone is invited! The Engel family thanks all of you for your prayers and presence.

Appendix | 161

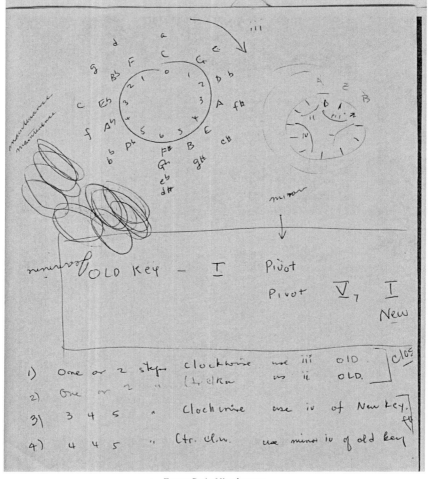

From: Craig Hirschmann

Cover from Richard Wegner's Score of From Heaven Above.

"Dick, Fond remembrances of our great years at River Forest.
You taught me a great deal. Jim"

From: Dr. Richard Wegner

Bibliography

Aufdemberge, C. T. *Christian Worship: Handbook*. Milwaukee, WI: Northwestern, 1997.

Bethlehem Lutheran School History. Milwaukee, WI: The school, 1984.

Braun, William H., and Victor H. Prange, eds. *Not unto Us: A Celebration of the Ministry of Kurt J. Eggert*. Milwaukee, WI: Northwestern, 2001.

Choir history. Lutheran A Cappella Choir of Milwaukee. http://www.lutheranacappella.org/choir_history.htm [accessed April 1, 2009]

"Classical organ planned for chapel." *Concordia Courier* 30, no. 1 (January 17, 1962).

"College Choir goes on tour." *DMLC Messenger* 70, no. 5.

Concordia chapel to get new organ." *Concordia Courier* 30, no. 4 (September 28, 1962)

Concordia College centennial jubilee, 1881-1981. Mequon, WI: The college, 1984.

The Concordia Hymn Prelude Series Index. St. Louis, MO: Concordia, 1986. Dedicatory organ recital folder, Memorial Lutheran Church, Glendale, WI.

"Dedicatory recital." *Concordia Courier* 32, no. 1 (February 28, 1964). "DMLC choir tour recap." DMLC Messenger 70, no. 6.

Engel, James. *I Walk with Angels*. Springfield, OH: Chantry Music Press, 1978.

_____ *A Manual for the Beginning Church Organist*. New Ulm, MN: DMLC Press, n.d.

Hallmann, John H. "First Zion Evangelical Lutheran Church," http:// pages.prodigy.net/johnhhallman/firstzionchi.htm [accessed June 11, 2010].

Immanuel 100th Anniversary. Milwaukee, WI: Immanuel Lutheran Church, 1966.

Krause, Carol. *History of Wisconsin Lutheran High School.* Wisconsin Lutheran High School. http://www.wlhs.org/4history.htm [accessed March 19, 2009]

Lutheran A Cappella Choir of Milwaukee, "Choir history," Lutheran A Cappella Choir. http://www.lutheranacappella.org/choir_history. htm [accessed April 1, 2009].

"Masters give duo-piano recital." *Concordia Courier* 28, no. 2 (March 21, 1960).

"New organ for chapel dedicated." *Concordia Courier* 31, no. 5 (November 30, 1963).

Northern Wisconsin District, WELS. *Northward in Christ: a history of the Northern Wisconsin District of the Wisconsin Evangelical Lutheran Synod.* S.l.: Northern Wiscsonsin District, WELS, 2000.

Obituary. *[James Engel's Funeral Bulletin.]*

Rejoice! What great things God has done for us: 125th anniversary of St. Peter Ev. Lutheran Church. Freedom, WI: The church, 1993.

Schantz Organ Company. http://www.schantzorgan.com/Recent Detail.cfm?yJob=2274 [accessed March 19,2009].

Tenuta, Marci. "Talk of the town: Piano teacher to receive a big thank-you for his years of compassionate instruction," *Racine Journal Times.* May 2, 2007.

Weber, Richard. *Bethlehem's Pipe Organ.*

"Who's new on campus." *DMLC Messenger* 66, no. 1 (October 10, 1975).

.